GOD'S ANSWER TO YOUR DEEPEST LONGINGS

Presented To

_____

By

_____

Date

_____

NexGen® is an imprint of
Cook Communications Ministries
Colorado Springs, CO 80918
Cook Communications, Paris, Ontario
Kingsway Communications, Eastbourne, England

A PASSIONATE LIFE DEVOTIONAL FOR WOMEN
GOD'S ANSWER TO YOUR DEEPEST LONGING
© 2005 by Mike Breen and Walt Kallestad

Contributing Writers: Heather Gemmen, Susan M. Miller
Cover Design: Brand Navigation, LLC
Cover Photo: PhotoDisc

First Printing, 2005
Printed in Canada
1 2 3 4 5 6 7 8 9 10 Printing/Year 10 09 08 07 06 05

0781443008

LIFESHAPES

A
Passionate
LIFE

DEVOTIONAL *for*
WOMEN

GOD'S ANSWER *to*
YOUR DEEPEST LONGINGS

HONOR **HB** BOOKS

Inspiration and Motivation for the Seasons of Life

COOK COMMUNICATIONS MINISTRIES
Colorado Springs, Colorado • Paris, Ontario
KINGSWAY COMMUNICATIONS LTD
Eastbourne, England

INTRODUCTION

What do you want from life? A husband? Children? Better relationships? A more meaningful career? Our culture is constantly sowing seeds of discontent in our souls, leaving us with the feeling that no matter what we have, it isn't enough. We long for fulfillment, purpose, significance—a red-hot, passionate life. Instead, the life many of us are living is merely lukewarm!

God knows what you long for; he's not a bit surprised by what you desire! He hears the cry of your heart and he looks past it into the deepest parts of your soul. He loves you so much that he will not always give you what you long for but instead helps you long for what he wants to give you.

You see, passion itself is not enough—the world is full of passionate yet misdirected people living hollow lives. It's about being passionate for the *right* things—things like choosing to learn from life-altering moments, maintaining a healthy balance in your relationships, knowing the role God has created you for and living in rhythm with life. It's about realizing how to be an effective leader, learning to talk with God in a more intimate way, practicing principles that enable you to live a vital life, and having a heart that longs to reach out to others.

Your longings as a lover, mother, homemaker, friend, daughter, sister, church member, employee, community member, and individual—all are God-given longings that are meant to bring great glory to him but instead might sometimes inhibit you from walking wholeheartedly with him. So what's the key?

Instead of asking God to walk with you along the paths *you* have chosen, stop and listen to God's invitation to come walk with him in the way *he* has chosen for you. You can learn to look at your longings from his perspective—to reshape your life so that the two of you are walking in sync. As you do, you will discover more and more that wrapped within your desires is the only One who can fulfill your deepest longings. You will find satisfaction, healing, and worth in the midst of your circumstances, whatever they may be. You will be living a passionate life.

How to Use This Devotional

*T*he devotionals in this journal are all based around the concepts presented in *LifeShapes*. *LifeShapes* takes advantage of our tendency to remember what we see longer than what we hear. Biblical principles connected to basic shapes help you remember how to follow Jesus' example in every aspect of your life. As you read these devotionals, notice that we have connected each to one of the following *LifeShapes*.

The Circle: Jesus marked the beginning of his ministry by calling on all believers to *repent* and *believe* (Mark 1:15). The Circle takes us through the process of repentance and belief and faith so that our lives can be fully changed for Christ.

The Semi-Circle: Every day, week, month, and year of Jesus' ministry was marked by periods of work and rest. He calls upon us to find the same rhythms of fruitfulness and abiding characterized by equal moments of work and rest in our lives (John 15:1-4).

The Triangle: Jesus had the perfect balance in all the relationships of his life, UP with the Father, IN with the disciples, and OUT with the rest of the world. We can live a balanced and relational life by following the same example of Jesus seen in Matthew 9:35-38.

The Square: Jesus is greatest leader of all time. And the fact that we all have at least one other person looking to us as an example makes us leaders as well. Use Jesus' example to teach you the four principles of good leadership and personal growth (Mark 1:16-20; Luke 12:32-34; John 15:14-15; Matt. 28:18-20).

The Pentagon: Ephesians 4 tells of the five ministry roles and that we have all been granted at least one. Once you discover the role God designed you for, you can stop striving to be something you weren't meant to be and do something that will truly build up the body of Christ.

The Hexagon: Jesus taught us the perfect prayer in Matthew 6:9-13. Learn the six phrases that Jesus prayed and what he truly meant by them and your prayer life will become the most effective and dynamic you've ever experienced.

The Heptagon: Biological life has seven basic requirements and our spiritual lives have the same. Practice each of them and your spirit will be renewed and refreshed with the presence of God (1 Pet. 2:4-5).

The Octagon: Evangelism can be a scary thing for those who aren't really sure what they're doing. But Jesus simply tells us to be on the lookout for the *Person of Peace* (Luke 10:5-6). Understanding this concept makes evangelism and discipleship a much simpler task.

For more information on *LifeShapes* and other products available, visit **www.LifeShapes.com**.

I WANT A SOUL MATE

"Your desire will be for your husband."

GENESIS 3:16

Allison dreaded her upcoming birthday. Just one more reminder of what she didn't have. Her girlfriends would come over, eat popcorn, and tell her how much they hated her for keeping her girlish figure—but then they would go home to their husbands while she climbed alone into her king-sized bed. Allison didn't understand it. She was a godly woman, lovely and pleasant, smart and interesting. Why couldn't she find Mr. Right?

Allison isn't the only one asking this question. Many women long for a husband. Maybe you do. You want romance, a life partner, a family. This is a natural desire, for God designed man and woman to be companions. So what is stopping you from having the man of your dreams?

There is truth in the sometimes painful advice of well-intentioned friends and family—God is the best husband; God is preparing you for each other; God's timing is perfect. But these platitudes don't meet the heart issue.

Why is this longing so important to you? Search your

heart as you spend time daily in the Word and in prayer. Is your longing from God or is your manhunt simply an avoidance tactic for some other thing God is calling you to do? If you are unclear as to what God's will for you is in this area, then you simply have to wait.

It hurts. But the worst thing that could happen when you're chasing after something God doesn't intend for you is that he'll allow you to catch it.

And waiting doesn't mean doing nothing. Continue to develop your relationships with others in your faith community. Invite them into your heart to fill the empty places and to guide you in the process of building healthy relationships. Look outside your inner circle for others who need

TRIANGLE

UP
IN
OUT

to know the compassion of your God. You will find yourself drawing closer to him as you share in the passion of his heart. What God has planned for you is much, much better than what you plan for yourself.

*Holy God, you know my desire
to have a soul mate. But today I'm
not asking you to meet that longing.
Today I ask for wisdom to know if
that is your will for my life. Amen.*

I WANT HIM TO DESIRE ME

"The things that come out of the mouth
come from the heart."

MATTHEW 15:18

Andrea knew he was married, but surely he wouldn't hit on her like this if his wife were treating him right. Clearly their marriage would fall apart whether or not Andrea received his advances. Besides, the way he looked at her made her toes tingle. And so she smiled back. But after the passion had passed, she saw it clearly: She was involved with a married man who wanted a wife he could respect and a mistress he could desire. She felt ashamed and trapped.

Of course, this would never happen to you! The statistics, however, show otherwise. And we shouldn't be surprised that it happens, even among Christians. As women, we want to be desired. Why else would we spend countless hours and dollars making ourselves beautiful? We want to be desired by the one we love and, in the proper context, there's absolutely nothing wrong with that.

The problem is that we're mixed up about what makes us desirable. Your attitude and behavior affect your outward appearance. You may think—and even he may think—that his desire for you is primarily based on attractiveness. It just isn't true. No matter how beautiful you may be on the outside, it's what comes from inside that really counts!

Watch for the next time you find yourself looking in the mirror to rate yourself. Is what you see a true measure of your desirability? Reflect on how you might spend your energy making yourself more beautiful from the inside out. Ask someone you know and trust what it is about you that he or she finds beautiful. Listen when someone pays you a compliment about either your character or your appearance, and accept it even if you find it hard to believe.

CIRCLE

OBSERVE
REFLECT
DISCUSS

And when it comes to men, remember: When he respects you and loves you, he'll desire you. If he doesn't respect and love you, you don't want him to desire you.

Dear God, Scripture says you had no physical attractiveness, and yet you are my beautiful Savior. Become the object of my affections, and let me know how much you desire me. I love you, Lord. Amen.

I WANT TO BE APPRECIATED

"We who are strong ought to bear with the failings
of the weak and not to please ourselves.
Each of us should please his neighbor
for his good, to build him up."

ROMANS 15:1-2

Michelle looked at her watch and began packing up
to go home. "Why do you rush home for your
man all the time?" her friend asked. "We're not living in the
sixties. Let him get his own grub." Michelle just smiled. "I
like to make him happy. I want to make him feel like he's
God's gift to me. Because, well, he is." When Rob came
home grouchy and complained at dinnertime that Michelle
forgot to put salt on the table again, Michelle was tempted
to run from the room and cry to her friend, "You were
right!" Instead, she chose to plant a kiss on her husband's
cheek, saying, "How do you manage to be so gorgeous even
when you're grumpy?"

We don't know the rest of the story. We don't know if Rob's face brightened as he declared Michelle the world's best woman or if he brushed off her affection. But we do know that Michelle did the right thing.

Following Jesus means we are called to be servants. Of course you desire—and deserve!—appreciation for your acts of service, but that's not why you serve your husband. You serve him because you owe it to him. (He owes it to you just as much, but that's none of your business.) Rather than serving your husband with the expectation of a return, serve him with the desire to build him up. And then take immense private pleasure in knowing that you're the one who gave him the confidence he wears in front of others.

SQUARE

LEADERS
SET AN
EXAMPLE

Precious Jesus, I don't think I fully understand what it took for you to make yourself my servant. Surely if you could do it, I can too! I thank you and I honor you. Amen.

I WANT TO BE HIS PARTNER

"In the same way, their wives are to be women
worthy of respect, not malicious talkers but
temperate and trustworthy in everything."

1 TIMOTHY 3:11

Gloria was hurt. Her husband, Tom, had come
home and announced that he had accepted a trans-
fer and they were moving. Again. She pushed down the
bitter tears she felt welling up inside her as she tried to
patiently listen to Tom explain why this was such a good
thing. Later, while talking with her best friend, the dam
broke and Gloria sobbed, "It's not that I don't think this is
the right thing for us to do. It's just that I wish I could have
been part of the decision. What's wrong with Tom? Doesn't
he trust my judgment? Doesn't it matter to him what
I want?"

It's hard to not complain about our husbands when they
don't seem to treat us with dignity. We want them to ask our
advice and take action on the mutual decisions we make.

We want them to respect our need for security by not over-spending, just as we respect their need for success by encouraging them in their work. In short, we want to be partners.

The truth is that, whether you and he like it or not, you are your spouse's partner. His choices affect you, and your choices affect him. You are "one flesh" not only in the bedroom, but in the church, the community, and the workplace. As you go about your daily life, be aware of the fact that everything you do has consequences for him. Good or bad.

CIRCLE

PLAN
ACCOUNT
ACT

How good a partner are you? The better partner you are, the better he will be. Ask him about his plans. Tell him you want to help him reach his goals; hold him accountable in practical ways while always being ready to cheer him on as he nears the finish line. You and your spouse can be examples of Christian unity and mutual respect in the way you partner with one another—and that is an example sorely needed in today's culture.

Jesus Christ, I take on your name as a Christian. I am honored to be your partner and I pray that you will help me to represent you well. Amen.

I WANT HIM TO BE THE SPIRITUAL LEADER

"Wives, submit to your husbands as to the Lord."
EPHESIANS 5:22

*T*racy hurried through her errands—depositing her paycheck, making a house payment, picking up her dry cleaning—as she thought of the delicious dinner that would be waiting on the table when she got home. Her John was the world's best husband, and she knew how lucky she was to have him. As she walked in the door, the kids pounced on her and dragged her to the dining room, where John pushed them aside so he could give her a kiss. They sat down to eat, John led them in prayer, and Tracy knew she would do anything for this man.

Scripture is clear that wives are to submit to the leadership of their husbands. God's Word is equally clear that the man is to love his wife and give himself up for her. It is just about impossible to submit to your man when you don't trust him to love you. It's tempting to put conditions on your submission—when he proves he loves me or if he shows he respects me, then I'll submit to his leadership. The turth is that whether or not you help bring home the bacon, no matter which of you is the introvert or the extrovert, and even if he isn't loving you as well as you deserve, you are called to submit to your husband. There's just no getting around it.

There's a saying that the only way your husband can influence the spiritual temperature of the home is if you give up control of the thermostat. If you're husband isn't the spiritual leader you want him to be, your disobedience in the area of submission may be depriving him of the "food" he needs to grow as a spiritual leader. Trust first in God, who made you an equal heir to the Kingdom with your husband. When you submit, you free him to grow into the man God designed him to be—and, ironically, you become a stronger and a more godly woman.

HEPTAGON

MRS GREN
NUTRITION

Heavenly Father, even when I disagree with or don't understand your ways, I know they are best. I submit to you. I trust you to care for me when I submit to others.
Amen.

I WANT HIS FAMILY TO ACCEPT ME

"Moses listened to his father-in-law
and did everything he said."

EXODUS 18:24

B renda dreaded the idea of going to visit Brian's parents and listening to all of his mom's judgmental
questions: "So you're really going to drive across the country
by yourself?" "Do you think the baby should sleep on his
tummy?" "Isn't it hard to be working full-time when the
baby is so little?" Even though they helped out so much with
the kids, she sometimes wondered if life wouldn't be easier
far away from her in-laws. The worst thing was that Brian
couldn't see it. "They're just trying to be helpful," he would
chide her when she complained about them.

We all hear the in-law jokes. Jokes like that almost make
us assume that we're not supposed to get along with in-laws,
even if they are wonderful people. The leaving and cleaving
part of matrimony can be dreadfully difficult and painfully

slow. How do we establish our own households and our own families while maintaining healthy connections to our past?

Whether or not your in-laws are cantankerous is beside the point. The thing is, they are your parents now. When you married your husband, you acquired them, too. It was part of the deal. And you know what the fifth commandment says about how we are to treat parents!

Living the way Jesus has called us to live is never more difficult than in the midst of family relationships. These are the people who know us best and often have the unique ability to bring out the worst in us. Be patient in developing your relationship with your in-laws. Building healthy and godly family relations is a marathon, not a sprint. Give God time to work in you and in them. It may take longer than you think it should, but God is not in a hurry and he is never late.

OCTAGON

PERMANENT
RELATIONSHIPS

Dear Father, thank you for teaching us the proper way to live so that we can give glory to you even as we find the good life for ourselves. Amen.

I WANT HIM TO BE MY FOREVER FRIEND

"In this same way, husbands ought to love
their wives as their own bodies.
He who loves his wife loves himself."
Ephesians 5:28

*E*lizabeth looked at the man sleeping beside her. He was snoring, and she had a clear view of his nose hairs trembling. He was bald, and even when his face was in repose, wrinkles covered it. She knew that face better than she knew her own. Elizabeth leaned over to kiss his weathered cheek, smiled contentedly, and then lay down beside him. Though so many people had come and gone in her life, this man stood with her through it all. She had lived with him more than double the time she had lived without him, and she was grateful for his companionship.

Sometimes we get intimidated by the word "forever." We know that a lifetime with another person is asking for trouble: We'll age, we'll get bored of each other, we'll have the same old fights, we'll take each other for granted. Eventually, we might want the excitement of new love; we'll likely want to get away from our partner's idiosyncrasies that drive us crazy; we may grow apart.

Now and then you may consider letting your marriage slide for want of something fresh and new, but in your heart you know you'll never be able to create with a new partner what you have with your old: history. Think about all the things you and he have been through together. Even in the tough times, even while you were fighting, you were making history and building a future. And though you might not have thought of it this way, growing to love him more allowed you to love yourself more too. Your spouse, your lifelong best friend, is a part of you.

OCTAGON

PERMANENT
RELATIONSHIPS

Everlasting Father, I am grateful that your love endures forever. I pray that your Spirit will be ever-present within me so that I may become more gracious, more loving as time goes by. Amen.

I WANT CHILDREN

"He settles the barren woman in her home as a
happy mother of children. Praise the LORD."

PSALM 113:9

Deana didn't know how to stop crying. The test was
negative again. Just last week she was promoted to a
stressful management position; this morning she won tickets
to see a band she had never heard of; when she goes to eat
dinner with her parents tomorrow, she knows they'll press
her to eat more food. She gets everything she doesn't want.
Deana couldn't even make herself feel guilty for being so
ungrateful for the good things, because all she knew was the
emptiness of what she didn't have. Deana wanted a baby, and
nothing, absolutely nothing, else could ease her pain.

Most women cannot imagine life without children. We are
designed to hold them in our wombs, and we are designed to
love them with all our hearts. Some women don't have the
desire to have children, many women have fulfilled the calling to motherhood, but far too many women know the
agony of that longing that remains unfulfilled. We read in

Scripture that God opens wombs, that God closes wombs. We wonder in embarrassed silence, thinking maybe we're not good enough; we wonder in anger at God's terrible sovereignty; we wonder in fear whether we will ever conceive.

Getting angry at God is something he can handle. You may want to read through the Psalms until you can't even see the pages through your tears—because David, the man after God's own heart, has articulated with great passion the depth of pain, and he directs his brokenheartedness to God. "My tears have been my food day and night," he mourns. But even as he makes accusations against Almighty God, he remains faithful. "God has forgotten me. Yet I will praise him." (Psalm 42.) David understood that he prayed to a loving daddy who was also *the* Holy King.

HEXAGON

THE FATHER'S CHARACTER

God was listening to David thousands of years ago, and he is listening to you today. Even when his ways are definitely *not* your ways, he remains faithfully and lovingly engaged in relationship with you.

*Heavenly Father, you know
the joy of having a son. I beg you
to grant me the same joy.
And yet, Father, not my will,
but yours be done. Amen.*

I WANT TO BE
A GOOD PARENT

"Above all, love each other deeply, because love
covers over a multitude of sins."

1 PETER 4:8

Maria's parents had not provided her with the best
childhood. Her mother had always been drunk
and her father had always been absent. As a little girl, Maria
had vowed that she would never do that to her own children. She had read all the books on parenting, listened to
the tapes, and quizzed parents whose children had turned
out well. And now, here she was with her first baby in her
arms. "I will always love you, my child," she whispered. "I
will always treat you right."

Mothers know the pressures of being a good parent—
whether we put that pressure on ourselves or pick it up from
others. We worry about whether we're nursing just right,
whether we've sent him to the right school, whether we're
pushing sports too hard or not enough, whether we should

let her date. When our kids mess up, we wonder where we went wrong. When they are hurting, we want to fix it.

You can evaluate yourself. You know that you pray for your kids, that you restrict their TV and computer time appropriately, that you feed them healthy food and make them brush their teeth. You also know that you get red in the face now and then, that you miss some of their soccer games, that you don't help out at their schools often enough. But no matter what you're doing right or wrong (or what they're doing right or wrong), you couldn't possibly love them more than you do. And ultimately, that's the only thing that matters.

SEMI-CIRCLE

ABIDING AND FRUITFULNESS

As much as you love your children, God loves them more. Between his love for you and his love for them, you can trust him to guide you through all the stages of parenting. Allow his Word to guide you and his Spirit to comfort you and give you parenting wisdom perfect for your family.

Father God, you love me so much that you made the ultimate sacrifice for me. Thank you for demonstrating unconditional love to me. Help me to model that same love with my children. Amen.

I WANT TO GIVE THEM EVERYTHING THEY NEED

"Oh, that their hearts would be inclined to fear me
and keep all my commands always, so that it might
go well with them and their children forever!"

DEUTERONOMY 5:29

Cassie was flat broke. Being a single mom was much harder than she ever imagined it would be. She had to work two jobs to pay the bills, and even then it was tough. Sometimes she wondered if she should downgrade their home so she could work less. What did the kids need more: food and shelter or the presence of their mom? And she could hardly stand it when she couldn't allow them a trip to the movies with their friends or to buy cool clothes because of lack of funds. She wished she could lavish her kids with all her time and far more money.

We all know the phenomenon of increased spending with increased income. It seems we always have insufficient funds, no matter how much money we make. If we only had a little bit more, we could sign our kids up for football camp. If we only had a few dollars more, we would take them out to eat more often. We wonder how other parents pull off buying so much for their kids—don't they have the same financial burdens we have? We just hope and pray our children won't grow up feeling short-changed, or worse, neglected.

HEXAGON

THE FATHER'S PROVISION

Perhaps spending money on your kids—or even giving them your time—is not what they primarily need. Scripture tells us that if you obey God, it will go well for your kids, and even for your grandkids and great-grandkids.

You can give your kids all the luxuries the world offers, but without your commitment to obedience to God, it will all be meaningless. Your choice to walk with God is the best gift you can give them, and all the other things will be gravy.

Holy Spirit, thank you for inviting me into a relationship with you and for keeping me in step with you. I pray that you will never let me stray. Show me those parts of me where I need to draw closer to you. Amen.

I WANT MY KIDS TO LIVE UP TO THEIR POTENTIAL

"My son, do not forget my teaching, but keep my commands in your heart."

PROVERBS 3:1

Lydia was horrified. Her son handed her his report card happily, saying, "I didn't fail any of my classes." He was right, but in her opinion, three Ds, three Cs, and one B was hardly any better. Even his phys-ed grade was poor! She couldn't understand why he didn't take pride in his work. He was incredibly smart, much smarter than she was—and she would have been horrified with only *one* B when she was his age. Lydia couldn't help but wonder what she had done wrong. Was she not pushing her son hard enough, or was he feeling too pressured by her high expectations?

When our kids don't do things the way we planned, we second-guess ourselves as parents. We remember them as tiny babies, when our dreams for them were unfettered, and we wonder, "Where did I go wrong?" When a son who could be a rocket scientist declares that he's not certain he wants to go to college, our heart skips a beat. When a daughter who wanted to be a pastor's wife gets pregnant before she's married, we weep. We see so much potential for our children, and we wish that we could make their choices for them.

You need to believe as a parent that God has an incredible plan for your child—a plan filled with hope and a future. God has a plan but it may not be your plan! Pray fervently that your kids will always walk with God—but whether it's walking into the jungles of Africa to spread the gospel or to walk into a business meeting to negotiate contracts is not actually your business. Rather than asking yourself, "Where did I go wrong?" ask God, "How can I support what you are doing in the lives of my children?"

HEXAGON

THE
FATHER'S
GUIDANCE

*Dear Lord, help me to trust you
with my children. Give me wisdom
and patience as you work out
your plan for their lives. Amen.*

I WANT TO PROTECT MY KIDS

"We know that suffering produces perseverance;
perseverance, character; and character, hope."
ROMANS 5:3-4

Bethany grew up in a loving Christian home where she was encouraged to be adventurous while still feeling safe. She had a good foundation for raising her own children and they were flourishing under her watchful care. When her oldest son broke his arm at the age of three, she wondered if she should have done more to prevent his suffering. But when her daughter began to fear going to bed at night, plagued by dreadful nightmares that left her shaken and inconsolable, Bethany silently wept. She had done everything she could to protect her precious babies, but had failed.

Unlike many animals, human babies are entirely helpless when they are born, and our God-given instinct is to protect and nurture our young. We all know that no one is immune to the pain of the world, but somehow we think that our kids are exempt, that we can protect them from all suffering. And we have to think that, otherwise we couldn't cope—our thoughts and dreams would endlessly focus on not being able to save them from harm.

Reality eventually hits, however. You are suddenly caring for a feverish little boy or comforting a troubled girl after a bout with school bullies. Or worse. And you feel helpless, afraid. You may question God's sovereignty or his goodness. How can God allow bad things to happen to innocent children? Once you get through the questioning period, you discover the profound freedom of turning your great responsibility of protecting your kids over to God.

HEXAGON

THE
FATHER'S
PROTECTION

God can do a much better job than you can, anyway. And when the sin of the world affects your kids, he alone can transform the evil into good.

Almighty God, I surrender my children into your care. I know that you love them even more than I do. Keep me watchful while releasing me from fear. Amen.

I WANT TO COMFORT THEM

"I am concerned about their suffering."

EXODUS 3:7

Mary's heart broke when her son-in-law suddenly passed away in a car crash. She wept not only for the loss of a dear person in her life, but also for the pain that her daughter now had to face. Mary knew that she could not do a thing to shorten the journey her daughter had to take, but she longed to walk with her along the road through this dark valley. "I'm here for you, darling," became the standard way she closed each conversation with her daughter. "Always."

When trials come into the lives of our children, we know the time for protecting is over, and all we have left is our comfort. We drop by to clean their house and to prepare meals. We baby sit grandkids and feed the pets. We offer prayers and words of encouragement. We shed our tears day and night. And even that is not enough. Our words and actions say I love you, and we know that is meaningful, but we also know that they still have to carry the load. "If only," we say, "if only it happened to me instead of her. If only I could carry her burden for her."

But you can't do it, and you know it. You can't even fully empathize with your children's pain. Only God can. And the amazing thing is that he does. He knows their pain, and he offers to carry it for them. He hears their crying, and he does something about it. He hears your prayers on their behalf, and he answers. You use every ounce of your energy to comfort your suffering child, and it is salve to your child's wounds. But God, with a glance, resolves the issue and redeems the situation. His kingdom power is greater than anything in this world and, it's active in our lives.

HEXAGON

THE
FATHER'S
KINGDOM

Holy God, for some reason you look down from your throne to cast your eyes on the people you made, and you hear their cries. May your name be praised. Amen.

I WANT TO SEE PRODIGALS COME HOME

"'Father, I have sinned against
heaven and against you.'"
LUKE 15:21

*T*heresa threw a party. Just like the father of the prodigal son, she went all out—with honey ham and strawberry cheesecake and lots of iced tea. Her daughter had come home, and Theresa wanted all the old favorites served so her baby girl would know how special she was, how important she was. The neighbors were invited, all the good people at church who had prayed so fervently, family near and far. This was a celebration they would all remember.

We quickly learn to prioritize when a child turns away from the Lord. That nose ring wasn't so bad. At least the older boyfriend was a Christian. Bad grades don't make a difference in the long run. The only thing that matters is that our children are right with God. And so we pray. We pray long into the night until our knees are sore and our eyes are red. We pray until our precious ones are home again.

It's hard to remember that the actions of your children, good or bad, do not determine whether you were a good parent. Certainly, your good teaching will influence them to choose the right path, or to turn back to the right path if they have strayed; but it does not guarantee it. You may have taught them well and prayed for them constantly, but ultimately your kids will forge their own way in life. Their path is determined by the choices they make, not by what you intended for them. And whatever they decide is a rejection or acceptance of their Creator, not of their parents. God's joy—and forgiveness—when they do come home is far more profound than yours.

HEXAGON

THE FATHER'S FORGIVENESS

Heavenly Father, soften the hearts of my children so that they may choose you to be their Lord. Let the rejoicing in heaven begin today. Amen.

I WANT A HOME

"My daughter, should I not try
to find a home for you?"
RUTH 3:1

Angela opened a box at the top of the pile and started putting the silverware away. She sang as she worked, thrilled that she was setting up her own home. She tossed the old chipped mugs her mother had insisted she take, and she arranged the pantry the way she wanted it. When she got bored of unpacking, she studied the living room and placed the furniture so the piano, rather than the TV, was the focal point. Every few hours, she stopped her work just to wander through her tiny but lovely house. "My very own place," she whispered as she ran her fingers over the walls. "My home."

Even those of us who are pioneers more than settlers love to have a place to call home, a safe place to rest from all our work. A place where we belong. The type of home and the location we choose reflects our personality and current situational needs. We may live alone or we may share with roommates or have a family. If we are young and single, a high-rise apartment becomes home. If we have children, a comfortable suburban house meets our needs. If we are empty-nesters, we are looking to downgrade.

Wherever you choose to live, you will have life experiences that you would not have elsewhere. Neighbors will enter your life and change your path. Trials happen specifically because of the location. God expects you to invest yourself wherever you are planted. No matter where you live, whether or not you own your home, make the most of it so that your life may be full of joy and a blessing to others. In your service now, you're preparing for eternal life in the ultimate home God is preparing for you in heaven.

PENTAGON

BASE MINISTRY/ PHASE MINISTRY

*Lord, you go before me wherever
I go. Help me to follow and find the
path of service you have for each
stage of my life. Amen.*

I WANT TO HAVE
A HAPPY HOME

❧

"Better to live on a corner of the roof than share a
house with a quarrelsome wife."

PROVERBS 21:9

Tricia snorted water out her nose from laughing so
hard. "Cool!" her four-year-old gushed. "Do it
again, Mom!" Thankfully, Tricia didn't do it again, but
she—and her family—did continue to giggle throughout
the entire dinnertime. They laughed about potty humor,
mimicked each other, responded to wisecracks, and remembered funny things about their day. "I like these people,"
Tricia told her friend on the phone later that night. "Of
course I love them, but I really enjoy their company, too."

We can decorate our houses just right and purchase the
right furniture, but we make it "home" only when we fill it
with an abundance of love and laughter. No matter how gor-
geously the house displays, no one will want to be in it
unless it's a happy and fun and safe and interesting place to

be. We don't want our husbands to dawdle at the office in order to avoid the chaos of home. We don't want to drive our children to friends' houses (or worse) because they are embarrassed to let others view their home life. We don't want friends to decline invitations to visit because they are uncomfortable with our families or even because they're bored. We want a happy home. A place people love to be.

For some reason it is easier to be polite to strangers than to loved ones. You may be able to keep that smile on your face at the restaurant, but as soon as you're in the car, you're all barking at each other. But the simple truth is you will be much happier if you're happy! You can make the choice to smile, and not only will you make the day more enjoyable for your family, but you will discover so much more joy for yourself.

TRIANGLE

UP
IN
OUT

Jehovah Jireh, thank you for providing for all of my needs. But I thank you also for blessing me so lavishly, far beyond the basics.
Amen.

I WANT FRIENDS TO VISIT

> "As Jesus and his disciples were on their way, he came to a village where a woman named Martha opened her home to him."
>
> LUKE 10:38

Rachel loved commotion. The more people in her house, the better. Kids hung out in the basement while adults were comfortable upstairs. Rachel loved an overflowing household and never begrudged a single penny of the oversized grocery bill that fed her weekend guests. She often said that her house wouldn't be home if she wasn't sharing it with others.

We sometimes tend to be like Martha when it comes to hospitality. We want to do everything just right. Our stress level before the arrival of company is off the scale because we're frantically demanding our kids keep things clean while we're busy making the kitchen a mess with all our cooking. It may be fun once the guests arrive, but it's not exactly festive for your family ahead of time.

If you like to entertain in your home, then you most likely have the gift of hospitality. You've mastered the skill of enjoying the company of your friends without stressing out your family. However, the spiritual gift of hospitality is not just about impressing friends with your cooking or decorating skills. It is about opening your home to whoever needs it.

It's easy to hang out with people who are just like you, but God calls you also to invite into your home those who may make you uncomfortable, people like that elderly couple who has no family in town, those fatherless children in your neighborhood who could benefit from watching your stable family, that middle-aged woman who's on the lam from her abusive husband and needs a place to stay for a few months. It sounds like a sacrifice, but you'll gain more than you give.

TRIANGLE

UP
IN
OUT

Holy Spirit, thank you for being present within me and giving me good gifts. Help me to discern how you would like for me to use my gifts. Amen.

I WANT TO
BE PROSPEROUS

"Lazy hands make a man poor,
but diligent hands bring wealth."

PROVERBS 10:4

Sharon resented her little house and old car. She would go to visit her friends and secretly take note of all the little luxuries they possessed. She couldn't understand why they took those things for granted. If she had even half of what they had, she would be eternally grateful. It wasn't that she wanted to take those things away from her friends, but she couldn't help wanting some of it for herself too.

It's so easy to desire wealth, to imagine that money will take care of all our problems. We imagine striking it rich by winning the lottery or being selected for a game show or having the dream job offered to us. We think that if we had an enjoyable job, we would be more motivated to show up every day. If we could go to the Caribbean now and then, we wouldn't be so grumpy. If we had enough money to take care of ourselves, we would happily share it with others.

Spending your time dreaming about what you don't have interferes significantly with going out to get it. Coveting your neighbor's stuff prevents you from enjoying the good things you do have. There is nothing wrong with asking God for good gifts and working hard to acquire them. But there is someting terribly wrong with focusing so intently on prosperity that your life swings out of balance.

SEMI-CIRCLE

REST AND WORK

God gives us work to do, but he also commands us to rest. In fact, the rest comes first in God's plan! Before plunging into hard work that may dominate your life, take some time to find out what God's plan is for you.

Have big dreams, work diligently to achieve those dreams, and generously share whatever God blesses you with. The more you give, the more blessed you are.

Jehovah Jireh, I confess that you provide for my daily needs. Help me to give up selfish desires and teach me to surrender control to you.
Amen.

I WANT TO HAVE HOBBIES

"Six days do your work, but on the seventh day do
not work, so that your ox and your donkey may rest
and the slave born in your household, and the alien
as well, may be refreshed."

EXODUS 23:12

Shenika worked too hard, but she didn't know what
else to do. She worked in a demanding field and her
career goals called for long hours. It might pay off in the end,
but in the meantime, she suffered for it. When she finally
made it home from work, she could barely get through
preparing dinner and cleaning up. As soon as that was done,
she would throw herself on the couch where she would stay
until she was nearly falling asleep and then drag herself off to
bed. Not much of a life, she knew.

We all have things that interest us, that we are good at,
that would provide us with needed respite. But we procras-
tinate on starting up the very activities that we long to do.

It's like exercising: We feel so good while we're in shape and we vow to keep it up forever—and then we quit. Or it's like praying: While we're walking close to God we know we're in the best place we could be—and then we slip away. Leisure activities that would give us a sense of accomplishment and joy and that would make home a desirable place to be present themselves as a time hassle, and so we don't do them.

SEMI-
CIRCLE

FRUITFUL
AND
ABIDING

You may not even know what it is that you want to do to find respite. It's worth experimenting with various activities to find out. God commands you to take a day off from all your work; the spirit of that law should tell you that it is important to get adequate rest. And rest does not necessarily mean sleeping or being still. Sometimes even the most extreme physical activity that varies dramatically from your usual daily routine is the most restful thing you can do. So take a break, and get yourself out of the rat race for a while.

Yahweh, you are the God
of Abraham, Isaac, and Jacob.
You are the God who never changes.
Thank you for teaching us
principles for life. Amen.

I WANT TO BUILD MEMORIES/TRADITIONS

"You Pharisees clean the outside of the cup
and dish, but inside you are full of
greed and wickedness."

LUKE 11:39

Suzanne sometimes wondered if she looked forward to Christmas morning more than her kids did. Even now she was lying in bed waiting for them to wake up and tear down the stairs to see if Santa had visited last night. She almost wanted to wake them up. But that would ruin the tradition. They were supposed to sneak down the stairs and find the cookie crumbs and empty glass by the mantelpiece; they were supposed to scamper back upstairs and beg their sleepy parents to wake up and look at all the presents; they were all supposed to rush downstairs even before they changed out of their pajamas. That was the tradition.

Traditions are wonderfully nostalgic. They help us to remember where we have come from. In fact, God himself commanded his people to set dates for certain feasts and to keep these annual traditions, well, religiously! We establish rituals for certain holidays, and if they don't happen exactly right, it hardly feels like the right day. We remember birthdays and anniversaries not only because Hallmark tells us to, but because we know that they matter. And the best places for traditions to hold their power is in our homes.

You may have a tradition that goes way back to the days of your grandparents, or even earlier. Before you observe that sacred moment of silence when the food is served on Thanksgiving Day, tell your children why you do that. After you all dash outside at the first snowfall of the year, explain why you keep that crazy snowball in the freezer all year round. Traditions are empty if no one remembers the meaning behind them. God commanded those feasts so that his people would remember what he did for them. And it's your job to pass the stories on.

HEXAGON

THE
FATHER'S
PROVISION

Gracious Father, thank you for displaying the mighty works of your hands in the lives of our forefathers. Never let me forget. Amen.

I WANT A BEST FRIEND

"Jonathan became one in spirit with David,
and he loved him as himself."

1 SAMUEL 18:1

Margaret flipped through the pages of her old yearbook until she came to the photo of herself with her three best friends. She smiled. Those were good days. It didn't matter what was going on in their lives, they always had each other. Everyone knew that they belonged together, and no one could break those bonds of trust. No one except Time. Margaret sighed. She sadly admitted to herself that she never had a friend like that since high school. She was friendly with her neighbors and she got to know people on church committees, but she never found a new best friend.

When we watch TV shows like *Friends*, we might start wondering what's wrong with us. Why don't we have friends like that? The reason is because we're so busy with life that we just can't make time to hang out in coffee shops to bond. That, and because friendships don't happen like they used to. In high school and college, everyone was in a new place, seeking new relationships. But the older we get, the more settled people are and the less interested they seem to be in pursuing friendships. These days, getting together for dinner twice a year is a sign of a close relationship.

But if you're like most people in America, you feel lonely. Even though you have no time to complete all the tasks required of you, you're bored. You want more out of life, and you don't know what will make that happen.

TRIANGLE

UP
IN
OUT

Do you want the short answer? Love. Not just romance, not just motherly care, not just family loyalty, but friendship. You're looking for another woman you can commit to love without expecting anything in return—nothing except all of her love back. The good news is, she's looking for you, too.

*Precious Jesus, I don't know why I
so often forget that you are the best
friend a person could ask for. You
know me, you love me, and you are
always faithful. Amen.*

I WANT TO DO GIRL STUFF

"Isaac brought her into the tent
of his mother Sarah."

GENESIS 24:67

Charlene answered her cell phone on the first ring. "Don't worry," she said without even offering a greeting, "I'm on my way." There is no way she would be late for this appointment. She and her girlfriend were making good on the gift certificates their husbands bought them a few months ago. Spa treatment. A whole day of pampering: wax treatments, instant tans, back massages, haircuts, manicures, pedicures, etc., etc., etc. And a whole day to chat endlessly about the important things of life, from scrapbooking to mall shopping. Charlene thought she had died and gone to heaven.

No matter what scientists come up with on the whole nurture versus nature debate, girls will be girls. It's in our genes. We want to priss and preen, and we want to do it with other women. In fact, I think that if we're honest with ourselves, we'll have to admit that most of the grooming we do is to impress other women, not to attract men. And men should count their blessings for this female bonding that women engage in: It saves them from getting in trouble for not noticing the subtle hair color change or the new jeans.

Joining your husband on a mascara-less camping trip may make you crazy, and he won't understand why. As a gift to him, go on the "vacation," and do it without complaining—it would even be in your best interest to try to enjoy it. But be sure to have a shopping trip scheduled with your girlfriend when you get home. God created men and women equal, but very different. And, trust me, your husband needs you to have the girl-time just as much as you need it.

TRIANGLE

UP
IN
OUT

Creator God, thank you for creating me in your likeness. I like what you've done. Amen.

I WANT GOOD ADVICE

"Let the wise listen and add to their learning,
and let the discerning get guidance."

PROVERBS 1:5

Ellena saw hope. Her divorce from the man she had adored for fifteen years was just finalized, and God had already provided her with new love. She couldn't understand why her friends were so afraid. "Conventional wisdom says to wait a year before you remarry," they told her. But Ellena wondered what a year was. A year from the time he emotionally disengaged? A year from the night he told her he had fallen in love with someone else? A year from the day he walked out the door? A year from the moment she heard the judge say "irreconcilable differences"? What was so magical about a year? Ellena knew that her decision had to be right before God, but she wasn't sure how much deference she owed her friends.

Proverbs tells us time and again that the wise seek guidance; but other passages in the Bible tell of people seeking counsel only to be misled. We call our friends to recommend good doctors and good books and good responses to tough situations, but we know that even our most esteemed mentors don't always see things clearly. We want to get good counsel, and may even be ready to listen to it, but none of the advice is the same.

Ultimately you are responsible for your own actions. Only you can fully understand your motivation for making the choices you do and only you will have to answer for how you have lived your life. Talking about your experiences—both the joyful ones and the sorrowful ones—with a trusted friend helps you recognize the lessons that God wants you to learn. It's not always easy to hear another person's observations about you, but it's worth it to grow to be more like Jesus.

CIRCLE

OBSERVE
REFLECT
DISCUSS

Holy Spirit, fill me with wisdom so that I may walk in step with you. Open the path before me that will most honor the Father. Amen.

I WANT TO LAUGH

"Blessed are you who weep now,
for you will laugh."

LUKE 6:21

rina didn't know if she was laughing or crying. But whatever it was, it was good. She was sitting in a dorm room, knees hugged to her chest, with three other middle-aged women in the middle of the night. They all whispered and giggled as quietly as they could for fear of their neighbors on the other side of the paper-thin walls. Nobody mentioned the fact that they would all be exhausted during the conference the next day; the only thing they were interested in was the connection happening now. "I strutted all the way through that building," her new friend was saying, "with that lovely paper-wrapped tampon sticking out of my pocket for all the world to see…" And they all roared into laughter again.

"I love to laugh," sing the friends of Mary Poppins, "loud and long and clear." And the more they give in to the hilarity, the more contagious the hooting becomes. Not far from the truth, actually. We can't help smiling when we catch the sound of a belly laugh even if we have no idea what the joke is all about. But when the joke is between us and someone else, the pleasure is even greater.

You may think that you have nothing to laugh about or that it wouldn't be appropriate for you to laugh. You may be in the midst of great suffering and suspect that mirth would only minimize the pain. Perhaps, for now, you're right. But the time will come when laughter is the only defense you have left. So don't be afraid to take a break from the serious side of life and enjoy the playful side.

SEMI-CIRCLE

BALANCE OF REST AND WORK

When you give in to the God-given urge to laugh, you will find new strength in your bones. And you'll want to do it again.

Lord Jesus, your words of blessing
to the downcast are words of hope.
I pray that you will bring joy
into my life today. Amen.

I WANT TO CRY

*"'Give me two months to roam the hills
and weep with my friends.'"*

JUDGES 11:37

Patsy knew she was on the brink of despair, but she didn't want to bring down her friends at Bible study. A lot of garbage had been happening in her life lately, and she was worried these wonderfully patient women would finally tire of her whining. She would if she were them! "Things are finally looking up," she lied when it was her turn to make prayer requests. "I just want to thank God that my trials finally seem to be over." Maybe she was unconsciously hoping they would press her for a more honest description of her state of mind, because she was disappointed when they moved on to the next person. When everyone closed their eyes to pray, Patsy wiped silent tears from her face so no one would catch a glimpse of her pain.

Women have the wonderful capacity to be both gentle and strong at the same time. We are in touch with our painful emotions even as we move forward in hope. Of course, sometimes we try very hard to be stoic and to ignore the internal pressure to weep, but in the process we only do ourselves damage. Crying is a gift from God. Especially when we use this gift in the company of others, we release the full burden of whatever pain we're experiencing.

You may despise the experience of crying when you're in the middle of it. And no wonder! You feel miserable. You hate the ugly noises you're making and can imagine how unsightly your face beomes. You feel vulnerable and self-conscious as you recall hurtful events. But when the tears stop flowing and the hiccuping ends, you have a new perspective. You've learned something from the experience, and you finally reach the point of being ready to put your hard lesson into action. The truth is, there's no quicker way to joy than straight through the tears.

CIRCLE

PLAN
ACCOUNT
ACT

*Precious Savior, it breaks my heart
to know that you wept so bitterly
the night of your death. I cannot
thank you enough for taking
my load. Amen.*

I WANT THEM TO TRUST ME

"The only thing that counts is faith
expressing itself through love."
GALATIANS 5:6b

Keisha heard through the grapevine that her friend had another miscarriage. "I can't believe you didn't tell me!" scolded Keisha. She couldn't help being hurt that she hadn't been chosen to be the shoulder to cry on. "I've told you over and over that you can talk to me about anything." But the truth reached up and slapped her when her friend gently replied, "Keisha, you don't really care about me. Even now, when I'm facing a horrible loss, you are more concerned about your hurt feelings than my pain."

We all like to think of ourselves as great listeners. We want to be the one people name as their great source of comfort. Perhaps we like their choice to turn to us because it proves that we are respected, that we have what it takes to be a good friend, that we are loved.

Which friends do you turn to when you are hurting? You share your burdens with the women who don't show off what they know about others, who allow you to share your concerns without inserting their own story or commentary, and who genuinely care about you. What does that teach you about the gift of listening? At such a moment, you can't think about how special you must be for being selected as the confidante, you can't privately gloat over the inside information that you now have, and you can't assume that you have all the answers for your friend. What your hurting friend needs from you is unequivocal love. She

TRIANGLE

UP
IN
OUT

needs to be able to abandon herself to her tears as you wrap your compassion around her like a blanket. When you become that kind of friend, others will seek out your shoulder. The funny thing is that you won't notice you are everyone's favorite. This kind of love makes you forget all about your own reputation.

*Oh Lord, my God, I love you
with all my heart, with all my soul,
with all my strength, and with
all my mind. Amen.*

I WANT THEM
TO FIND HEALING

"When Jesus landed and saw a large crowd,
he had compassion on them and healed their sick."

MATTHEW 14:14

Pam wept bitterly. "Oh, Lord!" she called
out. "Why? Why does it have to be this way?" Her
tears were not for herself. She was crying on behalf of her
friend whose teenaged son had just been killed in a freak
accident. Pam had met the boy only a couple of times, but
she had prayed for him often in Bible study when his mom
shared some of his typical teenager troubles. If only they
could be praying over issues of acne and homework and dat-
ing now! "Oh, God," Pam cried out in the privacy of her
bedroom, "bring comfort to my friend. Bring healing."

One of the risks of friendship is that we start to care for
another person. We feel her pain when she faces trials, and
we are deeply affected by the stories in her life. In short,
we care what happens to her. When we become close to

another person, we want to know the deep places within her. We are concerned about the things that concern her, and we long for her dreams to be fulfilled. And everyone has wounds. So as we grow deeper into a friendship, our hearts are broken for the wounds she carries. And we long for her healing as deeply as we long for our own.

Friendship may be a risk, but it's a risk worth taking. One of the beautiful results of caring deeply for another person is that our lives take on more meaning; as we give of ourselves, we become rich. Not only do we gain the loyalty of a dear person, but we come closer to an understanding of what God intends for our eternity.

PENTAGON

PASTORAL
GIFT

Father of all, rest your eyes on my friends, so that you may acknowledge their pain and bring healing. Thank you for caring even more deeply than I do. Amen.

I WANT MY MOM TO LOVE ME

"The LORD did not set his affection on you
and choose you because you were more
numerous than other peoples, for you were
the fewest of all peoples."

DEUTERONOMY 7:7

Samantha thought back to her first piano recital: She had practiced so much her fingers were calloused, but when she sat in front of that black, shiny piano and saw the auditorium full of people, she panicked. She couldn't remember a single note. So she put her fingers on the ivory and played an impromptu tune that had no resemblance to the song she had practiced so diligently. A few dreadful minutes later, she stood up from the piano to bow—and saw her mother, who knew the huge mistake that was just made, stand up to applaud wildly, her face beaming with love.

Everyone understands the need to perform exceptionally well in order to receive a blue ribbon or a job promotion.

But all of us want to receive unearned praise from our mothers. Somehow mothers can believe that we are miles beyond everyone else in beauty, intelligence, and skill, and we want them to communicate that motherly pride to us without reservation. Mothers blindly receive us into their graces whether we deserve it or not and without a hint of judgment. We want them to brag about us constantly without noticing that others are yawning. We want our mothers to love us.

HEXAGON

THE FATHER'S CHARACTER

You may or may not have that kind of earthly mother. But you certainly do have that kind of heavenly Father. By the blood of Jesus, a holy God puts your sins out of his sight and sees only your delightful, beautiful, loveable self. He's the one who formed you in the womb and held your fingers as you learned to walk; he's the one who gathered up your tears and who made plans for your future. He loves you lavishly, and you can't do a thing to change that.

Abba, like a little girl, I will come running into your arms to receive your lavish love. You give it to me freely, though I know the cost was great. Thank you. Amen.

I WANT MY DAD TO BE PROUD OF ME

"A wise [daughter] brings joy to [her] father."
PROVERBS 10:1

Karen's father took her by the arm and walked her around the entire office, introducing her to all his colleagues and employees. "This is my beautiful daughter Karen. She is the mother of my charming grandchildren and a successful businesswoman," began his litany of praise. Karen blushed at her father's gushing, but she couldn't help feeling pleased. She held her head up high and chatted happily with each new acquaintance, gaining more and more confidence as her father beamed. And when she left the building, her confidence went with her.

Little girls need their daddies. We want our fathers to teach us how to ride a trike, how to drive a car, how to whack a golf ball, how to run a meeting—and we want them to tell us we did a great job when we master the task. We want them to push us hard, calling us to excellence—

and then to reward us with their praise when we do the job well. Dads can believe that we can do anything we set our minds to, so that we believe it too. And that little girl inside longing for our father's approval will never grow up.

You may not have ever received that kind of approval from your father, but that doesn't mean you are unlovely, incompetent, unimportant, or unworthy. Your worth comes from the Creator God who created you in his very image. He's given you a personality, interests, abilities, learning styles—all the things that add up to your unique set of gifts. Whether you like to stay on a job or church committee for years or change activities frequently to launch new projects, God has prepared you for what is to come. As your heavenly Father, he wants to discover the gifts he's given you—then use them in the work of his kingdom to glorify his name.

PENTAGON

PIONEERS
SETTLERS

Heavenly Father, help me to look in the mirror today and to see the person that you see. Help me to live up to my potential. Amen.

I WANT MY PARENTS TO LET ME GROW UP

"For this reason a man will leave his father and
mother and be united to his wife."

GENESIS 2:24

L indsey was middle-aged, had lived more than half
her life away from her parents, yet still felt like a
child every time she went home. She had to admit that
much of it was her own fault—she reverted right back to
adolescent insolence as soon as her parents started lecturing
her. She cried on her mother's shoulder about every major
and not-so-major crisis she faced, and she begged her father
for money when she was broke. But much of it was also
because her parents just couldn't see that she had made
many good decisions in her life. They always had an opinion (usually negative) about everything and treated her like
she had no life experiences of her own to draw on. Lindsey
just wanted them to acknowledge that she had grown up.

We all know that parents are supposed to work

themselves out of a job. They are to give their kids the tools to handle life well on their own. Parents are supposed to encourage their children to act independently and to enjoy (or suffer) the consequences. But we also all know that parents have a difficult time letting kids grow up. They joke about trying to keep their kids little, and there's some truth in that. Some parents can hardly bear it that children who used to adore them simply don't need them anymore.

HEPTAGON

MRS GREN
GROWTH

All you can do to convince your parents that you are grown up is to act grown up. When they give you advice, listen attentively and consider its validity. When they lecture you, respond kindly to their concerns as you would in a debate with any peer. When they remind you of your negative childhood characteristics, respectfully ask them if they think you still act that way (and consider if they are right if they say yes). You are an adult whether or not your parents think you are, and as an adult, you are responsible to behave accordingly.

*Gracious Father, I don't deserve for
you to give me anything, and yet
you offer me the most precious gift
of all: free will. Help me to use
that gift responsibly. Amen.*

I WANT TO BE PROUD OF MY PARENTS

"If you do whatever I command you and walk in
my ways and do what is right in my eyes by
keeping my statutes and commands, as David
[your father] did, I will be with you. I will build
you a dynasty as enduring as the one I built
for David and will give Israel to you."

1 KINGS 11:38

Helen dreaded introducing her boyfriend to her
parents. She didn't have the typical teenager's fear
that her folks would grill her boyfriend to make sure he was
good enough for her—she had the opposite fear. She was
afraid that they would reveal themselves as the shallow,
detached, dysfunctional people they were and that her
boyfriend would freak out and never talk to her again. She
had avoided letting most of her friends meet her parents, but
she couldn't do it any longer. She took his hand, opened the
door, and held her breath.

Our parents are supposed to be role models for us. The

desire to please our parents is supposed to motivate us to an upstanding lifestyle. When our parents fail to provide us with an ideal to emulate, we feel cheated. Worse, we feel trapped by our tendency to behave as they did.

No matter how wonderful or terrible your childhood was, you are responsible for the choices you make. If your parents provided a near-perfect home, then you have more resources than the average person—not just financial resources, but the even more valuable resources of confidence, wisdom, stability, education. You have the opportunity to give back to the world what you've been given. If your parents gave you a dysfunctional childhood, you have the opportunity to break the cycle. And no matter what, God wants you to respect your parents.

Lord Jesus, you are the ultimate role model, and I thank you for living among us to demonstrate perfect love and wisdom. Help me to be like you. Amen.

I WANT MY AGING PARENTS TO BE COMFORTABLE

"Now hurry back to my father and say to him, 'This is what your son Joseph says: God has made me lord of all Egypt. Come down to me; don't delay. You shall live in the region of Goshen and be near me—you, your children and grandchildren, your flocks and herds, and all you have. I will provide for you there.'"

GENESIS 45:9-11

LaTanya glared at her sister. "Nursing home? That had better be a joke, girl! After all they've done for us?" But her sister wasn't joking. She had even researched a local home that provided the level of care needed while extending maximum freedom to the resident. As much as she hated the idea, LaTanya couldn't argue, not with the tiny income and lousy housing situation she had.

We are in a wonderful time when quality health care is keeping people alive longer than ever. The baby boomers are becoming senior citizens, and the elderly are soon going to outnumber the toddlers. In other words, our parents are getting old and we have to respond to their needs. Somehow we need to balance the needs of our immediate family with the needs of the people who gave us life.

Aging parents who need full-time care sometimes insist that they won't live in a nursing home. The responsibility of deciding how to deal with the situation is something you get thrown into without preparation. Talking with others who are in similar situations not only helps you to come to a decision you can feel good about, but it also gives you a sense of the larger community, the preciousness of family, and the sanctity of human life. Once again, your parents, even when they're old and senile, are teaching you valuable life lessons.

CIRCLE

OBSERVE
REFLECT
DISCUSS

Almighty God, I'll never understand how deeply the sacrifice you made for me hurt you. Teach me to respond to your grace for me with grace for others. Amen.

I WANT MY PARENTS TO BELIEVE IN ME

*"May your father and mother be glad;
may she who gave you birth rejoice!"*

PROVERBS 23:25

Kari had the opportunity of a lifetime. Her dream to start her own landscaping company was finally a reality—all she needed was to invest a few thousand dollars. Though she dreaded the idea, she plucked up the courage to approach her parents. "If everything goes as planned, I will be able to pay you back within two years." Before she could even finish the pitch, her dad laughed and assured her that no bank would ever make a bet on flowers, so why should he? He suggested that she stick with her day job and quit chasing ghosts. The conversation was over.

Our dreams and aspirations may sometimes seem farfetched to others. We're careful about whom we tell of these goals we hold so passionately because we don't want anyone to crush them. Some of the people we most desperately want to share these dreams with are our parents. We want them to help us cast the vision and perhaps even to help us reel it in.

You may be disappointed to discover that your parents are getting more practical than visionary in their older years. They are afraid that you will make mistakes, and they want to protect you from the consequences. And they may be right; you may be making a mistake. But that's okay. Don't be discouraged by their lack of enthusiasm. When God gives you a vision and you answer the call, you'll stretch and grow in new ways no matter what happens.

PENTAGON

APOSTOLIC
SENT OUT

If your dream succeeds, live in thanksgiving; if it fails, take joy in growing. When your parents see in you an attitude like that, they won't have a choice but to believe that their daughter has arrived.

*Holy Spirit, grant me the wisdom
to get involved in the things that
you are involved in. I want to do
what you call me to. Amen.*

I WANT
A HEALTHY FAMILY

"'For whoever does the will of my Father in heaven
is my brother and sister and mother.'"

MATTHEW 12:50

Delia dreaded the holidays. Everyone would be talking about the stress of spending time with relatives, the hassle of traveling across the country, the pressure of buying the right gifts for everyone—in short, they would be talking about family. And Delia couldn't say a thing. Her parents died when she was child, and she grew up in an orphanage. She delighted in the wonderful man she eventually married and their three children, but she never stopped wishing she had an extended family.

Sometimes it's difficult to love our families. Crazy Uncle Mort is still trying convince everyone the world is going to end. Big sisters get bossy no matter how grown up you are. Dad still criticizes your politics. Going home can some-times conjure up memories that are more than just unpleasant. Old wounds flare up. We experience new pain as incompatible personalities mesh. But family is family is family. And as much as we complain about them, we love them.

You may be surprised to realize that the Word of God is often directed at groups of people, not individuals. God addresses whole nations or whole families and gives them commands or promises or words of endearment that you may have learned to apply to your life on a personal level. God, however, designed you to be in a community, and the primary community he placed you in is your family. So whether they drive you batty, hurt you significantly, or overprotect you, God gave them to you for a purpose. He intends for you to live with them, to learn from them, to love them as you love yourself. Reach out to those closest to you on your way to reaching out to the world. Model the good news of God's love.

TRIANGLE

UP
IN
OUT

*Dear Father, you adopted me to be
your precious child, and though I
make so many mistakes, you've
never once regretted making me
your own child. Thank you. Amen.*

I WANT LOST SIBLINGS TO FIND FAITH

*"Watch your life and doctrine closely.
Persevere in them, because if you do,
you will save both yourself and your hearers."*

1 TIMOTHY 4:16

Shannon's favorite memory was of her older brother twirling her in the tire swing that hung in the backyard. They would finish their chores and homework, and then head outside. He twirled her fast and hard and she shrieked with pleasure; and then, when they were both exhausted, they squished together on the swing chatting about the mysteries of life that could be answered only with a profound awe of God. That was so long ago. And so distant. Now that dear brother had outgrown not only the tire swing, but also the God who made him.

People who know the love of God weep over those who don't, especially beloved family. It hurts the most when the people who reject the faith grew up in the church and know all the answers. We can't open up the Scriptures to them and watch them marvel at the revelation of grace they way new believers do. It hurts, and it is intimidating. Just as it is our fervent desire to compassionately draw them back to God, they fervently try to "enlighten" us. "Just because mom and dad believe that, it doesn't mean you have to," they say.

You don't have to talk all the time about faith with a sibling who has turned away from God. In fact, you probably shouldn't. What your brother or sister wants from you is kinship; focusing on the differences between you breaks the tie the binds you. Your best hope for your lost sibling is to love her back to God. As you patiently wait for the day God softens her heart, study Scripture so that you will be ready to answer the questions she may one day ask you. And never stop praying.

OCTAGON

PERSON
OF PEACE

Holy Spirit, I ask you to soften the hearts of my dear siblings who have turned against you. I pray that you will do this for their sake and for your glory. Amen.

I WANT TO GET ALONG WITH MY SIBLINGS

"A gentle answer turns away wrath,
but a harsh word stirs up anger."
PROVERBS 15:1

Marion knew her email was blunt, but she didn't have time to soften it. Besides, her brother deserved a little abuse. He had always been such a jerk; it was time she had the upper hand. She remembered when he used to hold her upside down until she called *uncle*. He used to let her almost beat him home from the bus stop, and then he'd knock her down. When she complained, he'd say she deserved it for how she kept messing with his stuff. As adults, they didn't fight anymore, but Marion had to admit she still resented her brother's cruelty.

Brothers and sisters fight. All of them. No matter how wonderfully the parents work toward building a peaceful household, no matter how many books they read on strong-willed children, no matter how rich or poor the family is, no matter how old the kids are, kids fight. However, even while they're in the middle of a head-on battle, brothers and sisters ultimately love each other. They stand up for each other loyally and band together when facing common enemies. And sometimes, just sometimes, they enjoy each other's company.

They say to ask for forgiveness rather than permission, but it is easier to prevent a fight with a kind word than to go back later to eat humble pie. Avoiding fights is an effective way to keep the peace, but the true method of gaining family peace is through forgiveness. Once you accept the fact that fighting will happen, even among grown-up siblings, the pressure is off. No one has to be perfect, but everyone has to be gracious. Show the grace and forgiveness of God in your relationships with adult siblings.

OCTAGON

PERMANENT RELATION-SHIPS

My Lord, you call yourself my brother. You have chosen to walk with me as a close companion. I pray that I will have the grace to recognize you. Amen.

I WANT PEOPLE TO KNOW WHERE I'M COMING FROM

"While Absalom was offering sacrifices,
he also sent for . . . David's counselor,
to come from Giloh, his hometown."

2 SAMUEL 15:12

Darlene moved to a new town for a delightful job. She made friends quickly at her new church and felt right at home. And then a colleague accused her of stealing an idea. Though she was proven innocent, the fear that she was untrustworthy wouldn't shake itself free from her community. People held her at a distance, and Darlene couldn't break down their defenses. "I don't get it," she sobbed to her sister. "You know that I'm as honest as they come. Why can't anyone see that?"

Reputations can be built only through time. In new settings, anyone can say the right words and even do the right things, but until we prove that we will keep this behavior up consistently, people will legitimately reserve judgment. It's frustrating and humiliating when we have to prove our worth. We want to be trusted, to be accepted for who we are, and to be treated with the respect we deserve. But the only people who can give us that with certainly, or to even safely give us the benefit of the doubt, are those people who have walked with us for a good portion of our life journey.

It's wise to exercise caution toward strangers. You may have been badly burned by imposters who were not who they presented themselves to be, either because they were just plain dishonest or because they couldn't live up to the high standards they set for them-

OCTAGON

PRESENCE
EVANGELISM

selves. So, if you are cut off from people around you, all you can do is live humbly, knowing that the only Person who needs to be aware of your blameless heart has walked with you before you were even born.

*Blessed Holy Spirit, I beg you
to let me feel the nearness
of your presence. I need a dear
friend; I need you. Amen.*

I WANT THEM TO BE ON MY SIDE

"If only you were to me like a brother,
who was nursed at my mother's breasts!"

SONG OF SOLOMON 8:1a

Brenda slammed the door shut when her husband walked out. They'd had another fight about money—who spent too much on frivolous things, who didn't get the electric bill paid on time, who "borrowed" from the savings. "That man is impossible," Brenda told herself. Then she called her sister. Before Brenda could begin her litany of complaints to convince her sister that her husband of five years was an insensitive jerk, her sister opened up the conversation with, "So, do I love him or do I hate him right now?" And Brenda burst out laughing, all her tension released by that senseless loyalty.

We don't want our family to think about whether they should back us up. We want them to irrationally and unequivocally side with us regarding any personal situation we face. They're not supposed to try to see the other point of view or, worse, to try to get us to see the other side. That's the job of friends and counselors and teachers and church groups and accountability partners. The job of family is to be loyal no matter what. Blood trumps logic every time.

It may be a little unfair to ask it of them, but when you expect senseless loyalty from your family, you're not trying to get out of your responsibility to admit your fault in a given situation. You are looking for that safe place to deal with the blow of pain that has come your way. You need a rock of security to stop your reeling. But, with or without your family's help, once you've stopped spinning, you have to allow the Holy Spirit to convict you of your own sin so that you can repent and make recompense. Every time you do that, your family will be more inclined to set aside their logic for you again.

HEXAGON

THE
FATHER'S
FORGIVENESS

Holy Spirit, in your gentle way, convict me of my sin and my righteousness that I may be at peace with everyone. Amen.

I WANT GUARDIANS FOR MY CHILDREN

"So there was no one with Joseph when he made himself known to his brothers. And he wept so loudly that the Egyptians heard him, and Pharaoh's household heard about it."

GENESIS 45:1-2

Lissette wept silently in her hospital bed. She finally allowed the truth of her situation to penetrate the deep place of her heart and wept like never before. She would never enjoy the smell of spring again, never be a mother-of-the-bride, never write the book she'd always meant to. But then her heart turned to the even greater grief: her children, who had already lost a father, would soon be orphans, alone in the world. "Oh, God," her heart moaned. "Take care of my babies."

No one likes to think of mortality. We especially don't like to imagine how our premature death would affect our children. But we have to and we do. Lawyers help parents make wills to place their kids with loved ones should the unexpected happen. Often we place our kids in the hands of siblings, believing that no one can love like family. Or maybe you have a friend who has been like a second mother to your children.

Families and friendships are imperfect because they are made up of imperfect people. You hurt each other in unknown ways over the years. But you love them all the same. Your kids are beyond precious to you and the idea of entrusting them to anyone is excruciating. But if you have to do it, the ones you trust are the very people who pulled your hair and teased you about boyfriends. You want the best for your children, even if you can't be the one to give it to them. So you depend people who can give your kids the kinds of relationships you want for them. Ultimately, you leave your children in God's hands, and no one can love them more than he does.

TRIANGLE

UP
IN
OUT

*Sovereign Lord, I don't understand
why there has to be suffering
in the world, but I know that you
are in control. Amen.*

I WANT TO HAVE A LIFELONG RELATIONSHIP WITH MY SIBLINGS

"'Lord, how many times shall I forgive my brother when he sins against me? Up to seven times?'"

MATTHEW 18:21

Natasha hadn't talked to her sister in almost fifteen years. She remembered what they last fought about—it was their mother's dishes—but she couldn't remember why it was so important for her to win. Why had she given up a precious relationship over a little bit of china? Natasha almost picked up the phone to dial the number she still had memorized, but at the last second she hung up. "No way," she told herself. "I didn't get the china, so why should I have to make the first move?"

Alienation between family members is painful for everyone. It's unnatural. Families are blood, and blood is thick. We feel the pain of separation in the core of our being, and that pain expresses itself in bitterness or anger or depression. Whether we admit it or not, we want the comfort of reconciliation. We may want it on our own terms (i.e., the other party has to reach out first and apologize profusely), but that doesn't change the fact that we still want it.

The valuable price of peace within the family comes with humility. That's hard, even if the other person makes the first move, but especially hard when the burden lies with you to make amends. You simply have to let go of the grudge. And the only way to do that is to turn it over to God. If you genuinely want him to and ask him to, God will release the hook of bitterness from your heart. Your sibling may or may not respond, but you will discover it is not your sibling who is finally free, but you.

HEXAGON

THE
FATHER'S
FORGIVENESS

Precious Savior, I accept your grace, your forgiveness. And to do that, I extend the same grace to others. Amen.

I WANT A PLACE TO WORSHIP

"Miriam sang to them: 'Sing to the LORD,
for he is highly exalted.'"
EXODUS 15:21

Ruth had only been in town two days but she didn't have any trouble finding a church to worship in. She could have gone to a Wesleyan church, an Episcopal church, an Evangelical Free church, a Presbyterian church, a Catholic church, a Pentecostal church. She could have walked a few blocks to a local church or driven ten miles to a megachurch. She could have gone to an inner-city church with a gospel choir, a cowboy church with country music, a suburban church with a contemporary band, a country church with traditional hymns, a Gothic church with chanting. Her options were endless.

In America we don't always appreciate the religious freedom we experience. Having never known anything different, we act as if it would be abnormal for our government to interfere with our religious practice. The truth is that many governments—of both powerful and weak countries, both in the present day and centuries back, both in favor of and against Christianity—have forced their people to adhere to certain religious practices on pain of death.

You have the freedom to worship God wherever and whenever you like. Without knowing the urgency of joining with other Christians in communal worship at every opportunity, it would be easy for you to take Sunday morning services lightly. Don't. Take advantage of this opportunity to step out of your hectic schedule. Step back from your obligations to family, work, friends, and ministry and step into the presence of God. In worship surrender yourself to God, then hear God's voice sending you back into the world to do the work of his kingdom.

SEMI-CIRCLE

ABIDING

*Majestic God, I give you honor
and praise. You are worthy of my
worship, and I offer it to you freely.
Amen.*

I WANT TO BELONG

"You do not belong to the world,
but I have chosen you out of the world."
JOHN 15:19

aitlin figured the first time she would darken a church doorway would be at her own funeral. She walked past churches all the time, but the lifestyle she had chosen clashed so radically with the culture of church communities that she hardly even noticed them. The day she got sick was the day she realized how alone she was. Her friends disappeared, and she became desperate. In a fevered state, she approached the church she used to fling cigarette butts at and was shocked to receive immediate compassion. A family from the church took her into their home and nursed her body and soul back to health. Kaitlin soon became a part of the church family.

A bar is not the only place where everybody knows your name. A gang is not the only community that provides a secret handshake. One of the reasons we love to be church members is because this spiritual family does what a healthy birth family should do and what a secular clique tries to do: provide belonging.

A church gives you more than the social setting of a nice group of people. Those nice people will love you. Unconditionally. You are not required to do a thing to receive their love. However, the more services you attend, the more people will recognize and greet you. The more you reveal of yourself in prayer groups, the more concern they will extend. The more involved you become in ministry, the more respect they will give you.

HEPTAGON

MRS GREN
GROWTH

Just as children thrive in a loving home, believers thrive when they come together to encourage and challenge each other in a safe place—a place of belonging to Christ's body and growing more like Christ.

*Great Comforter, thank you
for being in communion with me.
Help me to grow in intimacy
with you as I spend time
with your people. Amen.*

I WANT TO FIND SECURITY

"A horse is a vain hope for deliverance;
despite all its great strength it cannot save."

PSALM 33:17

Debbie vowed never to set foot in a church again. She would never be so foolish. She hit the steering wheel hard and then began to cry. "How could he have done that?" she whispered through her tears. She hadn't seen it coming. The head of the stewardship committee had been so passionate about the new building fund, and Debbie had caught the vision. Though she really couldn't afford to, she joyfully gave up thousands in support—only to find out a few months later that the committee head, a man she respected and admired, had been using the donations to gamble away his evenings.

The church gives us a place to belong. People in the church throw showers for us, brings us meals when we're sick, invite us to their homes for holiday dinners. After experiencing this climate of kindness and grace, finding out that even Christian leaders are sinners feels like getting kicked in the stomach. Messed-up people worship in church, volunteer in church ministries, even run them. We expect better, and when we're disappointed by the reality that everyone sins, we wonder if there is any point in belonging to a church.

As safe as the church generally feels, it simply isn't a perfect place of refuge where we're never disappointed. We strive to be like Christ, but we all fall short, even leaders or other individuals we respect.

We don't depend on the church for security; we depend on the One whom the church worships. Only by God's grace do we avoid the snares of the evil one. We're never so spiritually mature that we don't need the protection that only God can give. God alone is our refuge, and he is very safe.

HEXAGON

THE
FATHER'S
PROTECTION

*Rock of Ages, you are my refuge
and my strength. You alone are
pure and good, and I worship you.
Amen.*

I WANT TO BE A VALUABLE MEMBER

"Deborah, a prophetess, the wife of Lappidoth, was
leading Israel at that time."

JUDGES 4:4

"I won't go to a church where women are not
respected," Hannah told her husband. "We just
have to find another church." It was not a new conversation.
They went through the usual points: Just because women
are not permitted to be pastors or elders, it doesn't mean
they're not respected; if women are allowed to lead in some
areas, why restrict them from leading in others; every role is
an important one; no person should be disqualified from
any role she is qualified for. Hannah sighed. "I guess what
I'm saying is just that I want to be able to contribute in the
best way I can."

Whatever camp we land in regarding women in office, we
all understand the need to be a valuable member of the
church. Showing up on Sunday mornings is good, but that

alone does not make us feel like we belong. We don't feel like we belong to a congregation unless we are contributing in a meaningful way. A meaningful contribution means different things to different people: For some it's teaching, for some it's leading, for some it's praying, for some it's ministering.

If you are not using the gifts that God has given you for the sake of the body, then you will be frustrated. You may not even be aware of what your area of gifted ministry is.

Take some time to discern what you are especially good at, what gives you pleasure, what seems to fit your personality as a whole. If you are involved in the wrong activity, graciously work toward placing yourself in a role that better fits you; if you are not involved at all, offer your services for a specific role that you know would be a blessing

PENTAGON

APOSTLE
PASTOR
TEACHER
EVANGELIST
PROPHET

to you and others. As you give of yourself, you will be filled.

Risen Lord, thank you for establishing the church through your servant Peter. You demand everything from us and you give even more back.
Amen.

I WANT MY CHILDREN TO GROW UP IN THE CHURCH

"'Let the little children come to me,
and do not hinder them, for the kingdom
of heaven belongs to such as these.'"

MATTHEW 19:14

Skyler could hardly bear it when her teenage son announced that he planned to start going to church with his buddy's family rather than with her. Church for Skyler had always been a family thing, so her gut reaction to her son's declaration was to deny him the privilege of independence. Then Skyler thought about how her son could barely drag himself out of bed on Sunday mornings and complained about having to sit through boring services. Maybe if he found a church he enjoyed, he wouldn't mind going. And if he did not mind going, maybe he would choose to make the Christian life his own.

That Sunday mornings are family time is a lovely idea, one worth fighting for. However, if insisting on this risks our children turning away from the church when they are youth, we have to reconsider. Deeper than our longing to spend time together as a family is our longing for our children to be in the fellowship of the Holy Spirit.

When you look for a church, you have a certain list of criteria. If you have children, the quality of the youth programs is definitely on the list. But when you evaluate the programs, you have to balance the fun value with the spiritual value. You want your kids to want to be there, but you also want them to leave with the substance of the Word in their hearts.

HEPTAGON

MRS GREN
REPRODUCTION

When Jesus tells us to make disciples of the whole world, that includes our kids. What better opportunity could we have to reproduce spiritually? Keep your eye on the goal of God's kingdom in the hearts of your children.

*God the Father, God the Son, and
God the Holy Spirit, you have built
us in your image; you have called us
to fellowship with you. I pray
that you will keep my children
close to you. Amen.*

I WANT TO LEARN MORE ABOUT GOD

"But grow in the grace and knowledge
of our Lord and Savior Jesus Christ."
2 PETER 3:18a

Nancy had grown up in the church and figured she knew everything there was to know about God. She was sad to admit it, but she was rather bored with church because attending the services didn't feed her at all. But one Sunday morning when she was visiting a friend out of town, she found herself deeply convicted by the sermon given by her friend's pastor. "I had never understood that passage that way," she told her friend on the way home. "It makes me wonder what other truths I am missing out on."

The older we get the more we let go of the urge to learn. Even in our walk with God, it's easy to think that we have all the answers on faith, that no one can teach us something we don't already know, that the Bible has no surprises left. We've heard the old, old story so many times that we might skip reading Luke 2 on Christmas; we might dread dealing with the crowd on Easter morning; we might let go of daily time in the Word. Not that we like our apathy. We don't. We long for the thrill we once had about God, but it just isn't there.

You don't have to give in to apathy. Live expectantly, ready to discover new things about this impossibly complex Deity. Plumb the Word of God for new insights; it is not a static book, because the God who inspired this sacred text is eternal and dynamic. Trust that God speaks through the most unexpected people—even through pastors who are too young or women who gossip too much! They may not even realize that they are speaking God's Word to you.

SEMI-
CIRCLE

ABIDING

Pray regularly, asking God to help you to gain an understanding of him; he is often not what we expect. And as you gain a better understanding of God, your faith will grow in vitality.

*Yahweh, I know that you do not
need to explain yourself to me, the
works of your hand. And yet I ask
that you reveal whatever I need
to see that will help me worship
you more. Amen.*

I WANT TO WALK CLOSER TO JESUS

"'I am the Lord's servant,' Mary answered.
'May it be to me as you have said.'"

LUKE 1:38

Jenica had welcomed Jesus into her heart as a little girl, and she was glad for the personal relationship she still had with him. She often thanked him fervently for his saving grace and wept at his mercy and love. "But I have to admit," she told her Bible study group, "that I sometimes get jealous of those people who speak in tongues or who say things like, 'Jesus told me . . .' I love Jesus so much, but he never reveals himself to me in a deeply personal way like that."

It's hard to imagine that anyone wouldn't want to have a deeply religious experience that would eradicate any doubt of the sovereignty of God. We insist that we would always do what God wants us to do if only we could be sure of what he wants, and so we long for him to communicate with us directly. We know Jesus is the lover of our souls, and so we desire an intimate conversation with him. We want a personal relationship with Jesus Christ.

The good news is that you can have all that and more: You can have certainty of, intimacy with, and direction from the Almighty God through his Priest and Son, Jesus Christ. The bad news is that it may not happen the way you might expect.

HEXAGON

THE FATHER'S GUIDANCE

God's Word is one of the ways he speaks to us. It might not seem like a miraculous encounter, but it is the most solid foundation we could ask for in building a relationship with God. Through obedience, we receive deep conviction of God's goodness and recognize his incredible blessings. With that peace, you no longer need the miraculous encounter.

Lord Jesus, I surrender to your will.
Help me, Lord, to know what
that means. Amen.

I WANT A JOB

"She considers a field and buys it;
out of her earnings she plants a vineyard."

PROVERBS 31:16

Chloe straightened the magnet on her fridge that said, "Mommy: the most rewarding career I ever had." And then she ran upstairs to slip into the newly dry-cleaned suit she had prepared for this job interview. She couldn't decide if she was nervous or excited about pursuing work. She had been out of the field for so long, but the last few months of updating her knowledge (and her wardrobe!) had been exhilarating. "Please, God," she whispered, "please, please, please let me get this job."

Work is highly valued in this culture. From teenagers to the retired, everyone is looking for a job. Our situations, skills, and personalities vary, and so do the job options: We can job share, work part-time, work full-time; we can work from home, on the road, on-site; we can spend time in a cubicle, in an office, in a warehouse, outside, in a service area; we can be behind the scenes, in the public eye, meeting people one to one. Sometimes we have a passionate dream to land a certain career; other times we simply want to earn a few bucks. Looking for a job can be overwhelming.

But you may be more concerned with whether to work than you are about where to work. Sometimes women feel internal or external pressure to stay home and raise children. Nothing in the Bible, however, dictates that a woman should not work. Your desire to be productive is healthy and natural. God gave Adam and Eve productive work to do long before they sinned. Work was not a punishment for their disobedience. Long before they messed up, our ancestors were given the task of being caretakers of the earth, and that is one big job. As in every situation in life, treat others (including your children) as you would treat yourself, and your question of whether or not to work will be answered.

SEMI-CIRCLE

REST AND WORK

Creator God, thank you for giving me the gift of productivity. Help me to use this gift in a way that is pleasing to you. Amen.

I WANT TO
BE SUCCESSFUL

"Whatever is true, whatever is noble, whatever
is right, whatever is pure, whatever is lovely,
whatever is admirable—if anything is excellent
or praiseworthy—think about such things."

PHILIPPIANS 4:8

*E*bony took excellence seriously. As a little girl, she won all the spelling bees; and, now, as a high-profile lawyer, she won just about every case she worked on. Some people accused her of seeking the spotlight, and she had to admit pride motivated her to a certain extent. However, deep down inside, her true motivation was to do everything well. She liked things that were beautiful and admirable. Ebony knew she couldn't take credit for her overwhelming successes—she was simply wired to drive hard, and she didn't wire herself.

Some people are impressively ambitious while others are happily low-key. The truth is that each one of us longs to succeed; we just label success differently. Some of us consider ourselves to be successful only when we have earned our way to the platform where we are noticed by our entire sphere of influence—and the bigger the sphere, the better. Others of us base our success rate on how content we are. We don't understand the crazy passion for more, more, more responsibility when all we want is to be able to enjoy the evening on the couch with a movie and a bowl of ice cream.

If you lean strongly toward one end of the spectrum, it would be easy to judge those on the other end. But that won't do you, or them, any good. God has wired your temperament exactly as he intended. And the truth is, we all need both ends of the spectrum—first understanding contentment and rest, then working passionately at what God calls us to do. No matter what you do, do it to give glory to God.

SEMI-
CIRCLE

REST AND
WORK

Dear Lord Jesus, I'm amazed that you didn't grumble about having to become a servant. Thank you for doing the job you were called to with dignity and passion. Amen.

I WANT TO BE AFFIRMED

"Be careful not to do your 'acts of righteousness'
before men, to be seen by them. If you do, you
will have no reward from your Father in heaven."

MATTHEW 6:1

Jocelyn was asked to give a presentation at work.
She was thrilled! She spent every spare moment she
had, even a Friday evening, preparing for this talk, wanting
to impress her bosses with her extensive knowledge. "I'm
going to knock their socks off," she told her friend the
morning of the conference. Her friend laughed. "You go for
it," she said. "It's only a group of interns. I think maybe
there will be six or seven of them." Jocelyn was shocked.
And then she was angry. "I did all this work for nothing?"
she grumbled.

In a work setting, nobody spends their time making sure
others get what they're due (unless it's a punishment, sadly).
We all have to look out for ourselves. Even our supervisors
recommend now and then that we toot our own horns,
admitting that otherwise they'll never know if we're any

good or not. As humble as we may be, very few of us can handle doing our work diligently and effectively without anyone being aware of what we are contributing. We rightfully want to be acknowledged.

There is one other person, beside yourself, who will look out for you. The amazing thing is that this advocate can do a better job of discerning what is best for you than you can. He can make sure you get what he wants you to have. He has the ultimate authority, knowledge, and grace. If you dare to let go of your own meager level of control and hand the reigns over to this generous heavenly Father, if you choose to let go of your desire to seek affirmation from others, if you humbly build up others rather than yourself, you will be richly rewarded—maybe not in ways that you planned, but in ways that are far better than you could have imagined.

CIRCLE

OBSERVE
REFLECT
DISCUSS

Righteous Father, your purpose for everything is always to bring yourself glory, and I want to join you in that. You make everything good.
Amen.

I WANT TO MAKE MONEY

"When the woman saw that the fruit of the tree was
good for food and pleasing to the eye, and also
desirable for gaining wisdom, she took some
and ate it. She also gave some to her husband,
who was with her, and he ate it."

GENESIS 3:6

Shelby didn't want to sound mercenary, but the truth
was she needed the cash. "I am passionate about the
work of this ministry," she told her boss in her resignation
speech, "but I need to have enough money to care for my
family's needs. The other job has offered me almost ten
grand more than you can pay me. I am so sorry." She
thought the amount would surely convince him, but she
cringed at the look her boss gave her. "This is about
money?" he asked, incredulous. "Shelby, I thought better
of you."

We all know that love of money is the root of all evil,

we see how materialism eats at the hearts of good people, we know the temptations that the allure of wealth elicits in us. And yet we all need money. We need it not just for basic needs like food, shelter, and clothing. We need it for building churches, traveling to foreign countries to witness, paying for Christian education. Adequate income reduces stress and opens doors of opportunity. Excess income frees us to engage in excess generosity. If we are honest, we want good money.

Money in itself is not bad. Having the wrong attitude about it or using it poorly is. You can be a millionaire and still be a godly and blameless woman. You can be penniless and still allow the love of money to rule your life. With the right attitude, pursuing a job that pays well is not wrong; in fact, it may

HEXAGON

THE
FATHER'S
PROVISION

be responsible. But recognize where that great job comes from—the Provider—and know that even if you don't get the job, God still provides what you need.

Jehovah Jireh, you are my
provider. Help me to praise you
in every situation, in poverty
and in abundance. Amen.

I WANT TO DRESS RIGHT

"I have become all things to all men so that by
all possible means I might save some."
1 CORINTHIANS 9:22b

*L*isa stared at the dressing room mirror, wishing the
suit didn't cost so much. "But it's perfect for work,"
she thought. "Classy without being pretentious. Attractive
without being sexy. Interesting without being gaudy." She
willed herself not to think of all the things her mother
would be saying to her right now ("Being a good steward of
money means shopping at thrift stores," "People who buy
labels have no self-confidence," etc., etc.), and she took the
suit to the counter.

We all like to look good. We may have different ideas of
what looks good—denim dresses with sandals, sport outfits
with tennies, or T-shirts and low-cut faded jeans with platform shoes. The desire to look good is the same. We believe
that the phenomenon of first impressions is real: People

respond to us based on how they perceive us. Our confidence increases when we feel gorgeous, so we dress and accessorize ourselves toward being attractive. At work, especially, where so often our success depends on how people respond to us, we feel the need to look good.

Looking good matters. Dressing appropriately matters more. You may be startling in your lovely yellow sundress, but you would never wear it to a funeral. You may turn every eye in your leather pants, but you would never wear them to meet your in-laws. Even when it comes to the clothes you wear, put the needs of others first.

Do you have to look frumpy in order to honor Christ with how you dress? No, of course not. But you are the light of Christ in the world. Think carefully about what shines through your attitude about clothes and the choices you make.

OCTAGON

PRESENCE
EVANGELISM

Father God, you dress the lilies of the field, and I have never seen anything so beautiful. Thank you for your love of beauty. Amen.

I Want to Balance Things Well

"There is a time for everything, and a season for
every activity under heaven."

Ecclesiastes 3:1

*D*ena—the queen of organization and the model of competency—couldn't find the phone number to her daughter's school, and she started bawling. Just at that second, her friend and colleague walked into Dena's office. "Oh, sweetie, what's wrong?" her friend asked. "What happened? Did you lose the sale?" Through the sobs and sniffles, Dena managed to say that she just had too much to do. Familiar with stress-induced breakdowns, Dena's friend took over. She sat Dena down, looked up the number, and reached in her purse for a bag of M&M's.

Some women think they can do anything. More accurately, they think they can do *everything*. They take on as many responsibilities as are offered to them. You've seen the type (maybe in the mirror): She's the mother of three children (who all do musical, athletic, and recreational extracurricular activities), the chair of the education committee at church, the director of sales at a fast-growing company, the Martha Stewart of the social circle. Some women just don't know how to quit. Okay, none of us knows how to quit—but all of us know we want to balance things better.

You can take pride in the fact that you are a woman who knows how to multitask. It's a great skill. You can take pride in the fact that you are a woman who can accomplish great things (and a great number of things). But you can't take pride in the fact that you sometimes stretch yourself so thin that you can't do anything well. You don't need to do everything today—or this month or even this year. Take some time out; spend it with Jesus. Find out what he wants you to do. Then work at that with all your heart.

SEMI-
CIRCLE

REST AND
WORK

Dear Jesus, thank you for offering
to take up my load
and to give me rest. Amen.

I WANT TO INSPIRE OTHERS

"Only be careful, and watch yourselves closely
so that you do not forget the things your eyes
have seen or let them slip from your heart
as long as you live."

DEUTERONOMY 4:9

Megan had a dream job. She traveled from hospital to hospital around the nation teaching doctors and nurses important coping skills during stressful times. She had started up the program herself after seeing too many of her colleagues break down when a significant medical crisis struck the hospital. The training they had received adequately taught them to care for others, but not themselves. The hospitals loved Megan. With her inspirational insight, she became an instant success and soon a bestselling author. Years later, when she realized the platform was the only support she had to lean on, she wondered when she had lost her friends.

People hunger for stories of hope, desperately needing encouragement. And if we know how to provide that hope and encouragement, we will do it. We are women; we are nurturers. The more often people respond to the gift of encouragement—often in powerful and life-changing ways—the more apt we are to keep on encouraging. Women like nothing better than a happy ending.

If you are inspiring others with beautiful insights the Lord has blessed you with, be sure that your own story has a happy ending. It is easy to slip into simply basking in the glow of the attention you receive. Remember your original purpose. Help others to become encouragers as well. This way the ministry multiplies.

SQUARE LEADERS SET AN EXAMPLE

Stay humble before the Lord in all you do, and he will use you to inspire the world—you just might not know it.

Dear Holy Spirit, I pray that if my motives are impure, you will still use my words to bring others closer to you—and to bring me back to you. Amen

I WANT TO HAVE GOOD NEIGHBORS

"If any household is too small for a whole lamb,
they must share one with their nearest neighbor,
having taken into account
the number of people there are."

EXODUS 12:4

J udy was surprised when an African couple came to her door. "Excuse me," the husband said, "I want to buy the house next to you, but I wanted to meet my neighbors first." She really was too busy, but she invited them in for a cup of tea anyway. By the time they said good-bye, maybe two hours later, Judy had a new understanding of the word "neighbor." "In my country," the gentleman had explained, "our neighbors are our family." He might have meant it literally, but maybe not. And several years later, when the families were celebrating Christmas together, it didn't matter.

Location. Location. Location. The mantra of real estate

agents. We drive through a neighborhood and determine if it's good based on how things look. Maybe we believe people who mow their lawns are the right socioeconomic level for us; people who recycle are as responsible as we are; or the solidarity of matching street lamps gives us a feeling of safety. We want the place we live to be a place we like to be.

Most people rarely bother to greet their neighbors even when they're both at the mailbox at the same time. You drive out of your garage in the morning and into your garage in the evening without even catching sight of the person who lives next to you.

OCTAGON

PRESENCE
EVANGELISM

If you really want a good neighborhood, build community. Do things like borrow sugar, exchange keys, sing Christmas carols together. To have good neighbors, you have to be a good neighbor. And one day you may have the opportunity to tell your neighbor about the best friend of all.

Dear Jesus, thank you for teaching me who my neighbor is. Thank you for giving me good neighbors.
Amen.

I WANT THE WORLD TO BE A KINDER PLACE

"The servant hurried to meet her and said,
'Please give me a little water from your jar.'
'Drink, my lord,' she said, and quickly lowered
the jar to her hands and gave him a drink."

GENESIS 24:17-18

*P*hyllis was looking into her purse when the light turned green. A second later, the man in the car behind her blasted his horn and screeched around her in the other lane. But what really startled her was the awful expression of hatred on his face as he flashed by. She spent the rest of the trip trying to erase that image from her mind but couldn't seem to shake the mood of oppression.

We are a generation of uninhibited anger. We see it in road rage, certainly, but it plays itself out in other areas as well. When a fast-food restaurant messes up an order, an angry customer threatens the lives of employees. When couples have a marital spat, police come. We wonder what happened to the days when strangers said hello and mothers offered cool lemonade to the mailman. Wouldn't it be nice if we all became sweet Southern belles?

You can't sit back with your arms crossed and a scowl on your face wondering when kind people will show up. You are not the only person in the world who wants people to be nice. The truth is, others are looking for kindness in you, too. Start looking strangers in the eye to see if they are hoping you'll smile at them. If you wish someone would introduce herself to you, quit waiting and go introduce yourself. If you see someone with a broken down car on the side of the road, offer her the use of your cell phone. Kindness attracts kindness. Start a trend with your example.

SQUARE

LEADERS
SHOW
OTHERS
HOW

Holy Spirit, I pray that you will fill my heart with your presence so that I may bear your fruit, specifically the fruit of kindness.
Amen

I WANT JUSTICE

"And what does the LORD require of you?
To act justly and to love mercy and to
walk humbly with your God."

MICAH 6:8

Janet was shocked to see the state of her home. "We let them live in our house for free, and we come back to this?" Their houseguests of three months had moved out the day before Janet and her husband returned; however, they left trash in every room, the oven was dented, the carpet was ripped up in the corner of the living room, and a window was cracked. "How could anyone do this!" she demanded of her husband, who, of course, had no answer. Janet's shock quickly turned to anger. "All I can say is that they'd better pay up!"

Life is not perfect. Far from it. People do stupid—even evil—things all the time, and we're often the ones who have to bear the consequences. The last thing we want to do is forgive. We want justice. Furthermore, we don't want to always sweep up other people's problems, not only because it is tiresome for us, but because we know that we may simply be enabling those people to continue in their destructive ways. We want them to deal with their own consequences so that they will learn a lesson and we will be recompensed for the wrong done to us.

How do we balance grace and justice? The answer is easy, but living it out is very difficult. We do exactly what Scripture tells us to do: We forgive. God has forgiven every sin we commit. Now it's our turn. We forgive completely and forever any and every sin committed against us—

whether it is as simple as a forgotten item from the grocery list or as painful as rape. But we don't forget, not right away. We hold that person accountable for his or her actions in a gentle and loving way, treating the sinner as we would like to be treated—the way God himself has treated us.

HEXAGON

THE
FATHER'S
FORGIVENESS

Precious Jesus, thank you for
forgiving me over and over again.
Help me to learn from my mistakes.
Amen.

I WANT TO INFLUENCE POLITICS

"Then the woman went to all the people
with her wise advice."
2 SAMUEL 20:22a

Diane maneuvered her way through heavy traffic, found a parking spot, and walked a few blocks to the courthouse. She remembered how nervous she used to get when being asked to openly discuss her own views; now she realized she must have been intimidated, because this really wasn't difficult at all. And it was worth it! She, like every other citizen in the country, was invited to voice her opinion on any subject to help the administration make a decision on an impending bill. She often took advantage of this privilege by researching the subject and carefully choosing the words she would use to articulate her view. Whether the verdict went her way or not, Diane felt powerful.

We grumble about the government probably more than anything else. We get upset when abortion laws go against our convictions, when educational decisions aren't best for our kids, when legislators pass bills that negatively influence our lives. We want things the way we want them, and we express our opinions to anyone who will listen.

The thing is, you need to express your opinion to the people it matters to most—that is, the people elected to represent you. If you want to make a difference, do it with wisdom and graciousness. Speaking out of passion alone, without information to back up your view, gives the opposition fodder to disparage your case. Learn from leaders you respect how to make a difference in a constructive way.

SQUARE

LEARNERS
WATCH
AND
FOLLOW

Precious Jesus, thank you for showing so much compassion to the poor and oppressed. Help me to fight for people who can't fight for themselves. Amen.

I WANT TO LEAVE A LEGACY

"'Grant that one of these two sons of mine
may sit at your right and the other
at your left in your kingdom.'"

MATTHEW 20:21

Amber wasn't seeking a ministry; she sort of fell into one. Friends starting coming home from school with her kids, and when others heard about her fabulous brownies and sense of humor, more kids starting showing up. When one little girl asked a question about schoolwork, Amber told her to haul out her homework so they could figure it out together. Soon, all the kids in the neighborhood knew that Amber's home was open for great fun, good food, help with homework, and a shoulder to cry on. "Mom," her daughter said one day. "I'm going to be an after-school parent when I grow up."

We all want to make a difference, to leave something significant in the world after we're gone. Whether we articulate this dream or not, what we are looking for is to leave a legacy. And that makes sense: After all, we are designed to hunger for eternity. Clearly, hungering for the eternal doesn't just mean that we're looking forward to heaven; it also means that leaving something of beauty behind.

SQUARE

LEADERS
TEACH
OTHERS
TO LEAD

The good news is that you don't have to write a book or found an organization or make history in order to leave your mark in the world. Sometimes the most powerful marks you make happen in a much more sub-tle way. Your legacy may simply be the love you allow even one person to experience; and whether or not that person grows up to change the world, you've made all the difference in God's eyes. And that's all that matters.

Holy Spirit, I pray that you will reveal my calling to me—that you will show me what I am gifted at and that you will quicken my heart in a specific area. Amen.

I WANT TO TRAVEL THE WORLD

"The whole world sought audience with Solomon
to hear the wisdom God had put in his heart."

1 KINGS 10:24

Leah had a camera in her hand, a visor on her head, and a smile on her face. She knew she looked like a tourist, but she didn't care. She was a tourist! She had always wanted to travel, and now it was finally happening: Buckingham Palace, the British Airways London Eye, Oxford Street shopping, *Les Miserables* at the Queen's Theatre, Victoria Station . . . So many places she had read about, and now she got to experience for herself. She knew her life would never be the same, and she wondered where she would go next.

The desire to travel often stems from a desire to learn more, to expand our horizons, to experience a new type of beauty. The travel bug is not a new thing. People had serious cases of this "disease" long before airplanes were invented. This disease is what sent Christopher Columbus off to discover new places; it's what drives young adults to college far away from home; it's what caused so much exploring that now the entire world is called a village.

When you travel you get a bigger picture of the world; you see it from a whole new perspective, especially if you go to cultures entirely different from your own. You may start to question things that used to make sense to you, thus growing significantly wiser. Having a well-rounded worldview can certainly help you to be more compassionate. Experiencing the world beyond your comfortable borders reveals the need for evangelizing the world more than just about anything else. When you travel, look for opportunities to share the good news with people who need to hear it most.

TRIANGLE

UP
IN
OUT

*King of Kings, show me the world
of your love so that I can show it
wherever I go. Amen.*

I WANT WORLD PEACE

"But in keeping with his promise we are looking
forward to a new heaven and a new earth,
the home of righteousness."

2 PETER 3:13

Kim was utterly serious when she stated her ultimate
dream. Everyone else had given wacky answers—
like they wanted to be taller or they wished they could walk
on the moon or they wanted snow to be warm. Her answer
wasn't any more of a stretch than theirs: Kim wanted total
peace in the world. Maybe it was the way she said it, but
they all laughed. "You should be Miss America!" one of her
friends managed to say between giggles. Kim stood up with
her hands on her hips and glared at them. They didn't stop
laughing. So Kim picked up a pillow and started the battle
for world peace.

Of course we want world peace. And it's not just pretty
girls on stage who feel this way. Whole religions are based
on the concept of working toward utopia. As human

beings, we want to believe that we can eradicate the evil in us and around us so that only the goodness in the world is visible. We long for the day when suffering and pain from our own mistakes and those of others no longer have a place. A new earth. It's an admirable goal.

We live in a broken, corrupt world where sin is rampant. But we also live in God's kingdom—not just in the future in heaven, but right now.

Jesus taught his disciples to pray for God's will to be done on earth as it is in heaven. When we share the good news of Jesus with others, we're building God's kingdom. One person at a time, we learn to pray for God's will to be done on earth. And surely that includes world peace.

HEXAGON

THE
FATHER'S
KINGDOM

*Heavenly Father, even as I wait
for your return, help me to care
deeply for this earth you placed me
on and for the people you placed
here with me. Amen.*

I WANT MORE ME-TIME

"I try to please everybody in every way. For I am
not seeking my own good but the good of many,
so that they may be saved."

1 CORINTHIANS 10:33

Melody voraciously read every self-help book she
could find. And all the books said that she needed
me-time, that she needed to take care of herself before she
could take care of others: If Mamma ain't happy, ain't nobody
happy. Her me-time began with a workout program, and she
was delighted by the results. However, after awhile, she realized a workout was just that: work—and she didn't think it
counted as me-time. She joined a Bible study and loved it,
but soon called that God-time, not me-time. Shopping
became a requirement in her mind, not a diversion. Before
long, Melody was entirely self-focused, but she still believed
she wasn't doing a thing for herself.

It is certainly important to value ourselves. The Bible says
to love our neighbor as ourselves—so clearly, having an infe-
riority complex is not what God designed for us. And it's true

that we need to take care of ourselves: physically, spiritually, mentally, emotionally. Enjoying life is not a sin; to engage yourself fully in the great gifts God has given you is exactly what he wants for you. Being the nurturers that women are, we need to be reminded not to put our own needs aside. We need to be reminded to take me-time so that we will be healthy and balanced.

You may consider grocery shopping without the kids to be quality me-time, or you may grumble when you have to get off the couch to throw a TV dinner in the microwave. We don't all get our inner fuel from the same activities. The important thing is to discover what refreshes you so you can serve others generously and eagerly.

SEMI-
CIRCLE

REST AND
WORK

Holy Spirit, I ask you to lead me to sacrifice my life in a way that is pleasing to you, beneficial to others, and fulfilling to me. Amen.

131

I WANT TO HEAL

"When a woman has her regular flow of blood,
the impurity of her monthly period
will last seven days."
LEVITICUS 15:19

Lynn dreaded going home. She hadn't been in her parents' house for fifteen years but had finally given in to the encouragement of her husband. "You are ready to face this, Lynn. I know you are. You are stronger than you think." And he was right. She went into the rooms where her uncle had molested her, and she was okay. She apologized to her mother for staying away so long, and her mom did more than forgive: Her mother apologized for the first time for not protecting her better. Lynn was amazed at the complete healing God had done in her life, and going home only confirmed it.

We all have wounds. Some wounds are deeper than others, but all take time to heal. Sometimes we think that our pain has disappeared, that we are normal again, and then it suddenly rears its ugly head at times we least expect it.

Other times we assume that this trauma is something we will never recover from, only to discover some time later that we are laughing again, that we went for a whole hour or a whole day or a whole year without thinking about the pain. And we laugh, because healing is never what we expect.

You cannot heal by ignoring your pain. You may start in denial, but if you ignore your pain or deny its consequences, the pain will become toxic and dangerous. Don't be afraid of the powerful emotions that will likely rush up on you. Work through them as long as you need to until you can move into the next stage of recovery. Forgive yourself for the mistakes you've made and for not healing "fast enough." Laugh as much as possible, cry whenever you have to. And lean on the Lord and the community he provided you with. Healing will come to you.

HEPTAGON

MRS GREN
EXCRETION

*Dear Jesus, thank you for loving
me and understanding my pain.
Thank you most of all for saving me
from my sins so that I can live
in perfect wholeness with you
for eternity. Amen.*

I WANT TO BE SELF-CONFIDENT

"Surely you will summon nations you know not, and
nations that do not know you will hasten to you,
because of the LORD your God, the Holy One of
Israel, for he has endowed you with splendor."

ISAIAH 55:5

Josie stood in the doorway and perused the room; she
realized she didn't know anyone. She almost slipped
back out, but a woman walked up behind her. "Hi," the
woman whispered. "I'm glad I'm not the only one who's
late." Josie smiled unconvincingly. "I don't know a soul here,
do you?" the woman continued. Josie told her no, and her
new friend smiled with such pleasure, Josie felt like she had
said something profound. "Come on, then," the woman
insisted. "Since we don't have to worry about our reputations
here, let's go make some trouble in the back of the room."
She laughed and grabbed Josie by the arm.

Even extroverts say they are shy at times. No matter how
outgoing we are, it takes a whole lot of self-confidence to
meet new people, to go to new places, to start new jobs,

to experience new things. Self-confidence is based on the belief that we can handle whatever comes our way. In new situations, we simply cannot predict how things will go, and so our confidence level decreases. The question is, how do we muster up that first bit of confidence to get us going on the right path?

Your confidence has to be based on something. You can't say (with integrity) "I am the best ballplayer in town" if you've never played. You have to build up the skills and physical strength to be able to walk onto the field expecting to win. If you want to feel confident about making friends, you have to know that you have a lot to offer them.

TRIANGLE

UP
IN
OUT

God created you. You belong to him. What better foundation is there for self-confidence? When you are confident of this truth, you're ready to reach out around you with the encouragement and inspiration people need.

Holy Father, I place my confidence in you. I know that you created me in your image, and for that reason alone I have great worth. Amen.

I WANT TO HAVE FUN

"Let him kiss me with the kisses of his mouth—
for your love is more delightful than wine."
SONG OF SOLOMON 1:2

Jaimie grabbed her sports bag and ran out the door. The house was a wreck, but tonight, she told herself, was the time to have fun. She arrived at her friends' farm a little before dusk. A bonfire was blazing, kids were plucking raspberries off a nearby bush, some of her friends were throwing a ball around, others were strategically placing a few kerosene lamps around the picnic tables. Jaimie guessed that some card games were in order. She sighed happily and ran over to help set up the tetherball pole.

Many Christians have consciously or unconsciously learned that fun is inherently wrong. It's not just that they're afraid of the traditionally "evil" things like alcohol, dancing, card games, rock music, and the like—they seem to be afraid of fun in general. Fun just isn't good stewardship of our time. Shouldn't we be working for the Lord? If we're having fun, we often assume it is wrong, and so being a

Christian feels like a burden. We wonder if it is worth giving up all the things we love to do just to live a Christian life.

You can have fun and be a Christian at the same time. God calls you to live a holy life, and that is not something you can fudge on. But a holy life may be different than what you expect. God created Adam and Eve on the sixth day, and on the seventh—the first full day for humans—everybody took a break. God had work for Adam and Eve to do, but first came rest. First came relaxing. First came fun.

SEMI-CIRCLE

REST AND WORK

Have you ever noticed how taking some time out for fun rejuvenates you? After resting, you're ready for the work God gives you to do. God knows your heart, and he wants you to delight in the life he gave you.

Dear Lord, I will obey you completely and fully. Your law brings me joy. Thank you for teaching me to live a virtuous life. Amen.

I WANT TO LOSE WEIGHT

"You women who are so complacent, rise up and listen to me; you daughters who feel secure, hear what I have to say! In little more than a year you who feel secure will tremble."

ISAIAH 32:9-10

Joyce couldn't help noticing the trim women jogging around the field at her son's soccer game. No love handles, no jiggly arms, no drooping belly. Joyce had to admit she was jealous, but she really didn't want to take up running. "Ah, maybe I will," she said to herself. "I've got to do something about this." She imagined herself in a cute little sweat suit with her hair up in a ponytail. All her clothes would look good on her and she wouldn't be so tired all the time. Then, maybe, her life would be good.

Look at women's magazines, and you'll see you're not the only one who wants to lose weight. It's an epidemic. Many of us are carrying around too many pounds. We're not being healthy in our diet or exercise. But we also want to lose weight because all those magazines show women who are unhealthily thin. We can't help wanting to look like them, but we can't (and shouldn't) compete. We feel worse and worse about ourselves, and we spend way too much time comparing our bodies to theirs.

You can lose weight. Really, there is no secret. You simply have to eat less and exercise more. So what's stopping you? Could it be that you really do prefer a nice bowl of ice cream to slender hips? Could it be that a good novel trumps muscular calves? Be brutally honest with yourself, and then live accordingly. And, no matter what, quit being jealous of other people's bodies. In these tenuous times, we all need each other too much to let a little (or a lot) of fat get in the way.

HEPTAGON

MRS GREN
NUTRITION

Holy Jesus, help me not to become so complacent that I expend my energy wishing for a new body rather than a just world. Amen.

I WANT TO GET OUT OF DEBT

"Give everyone what you owe him: If you owe
taxes, pay taxes; if revenue, then revenue; if
respect, then respect; if honor, then honor."

ROMANS 13:7

Francine stared at her checkbook. "How could I have
spent that much again this month?" she asked herself.
She had such great goals to be on a serious spending-freeze
and then to make extra-large loan payments. If she did that
for just eight or nine months, she would be able to stabilize
her finances. She had dropped a few bucks for a restaurant
outing with a friend, she bought a new blouse here, she
replaced a lamp there. How would she ever reach her far-
reaching financial aspirations if she couldn't even meet her
easy short-term goals?

America is in debt, and not just the government. Personal
debt has reached an all-time high, and it looks as though it
will continue to skyrocket. People want what they want, and

they get it whether or not they can afford it. Even kids are taking out loans! Owing money—whether to a bank, a collection agency, or to parents—is stressful. If we don't make monthly payments on time, so much is at stake: our credit rating, our collateral—sometimes our relationships.

You may have legitimate reason for being in debt. Health bills might have driven you to depend on a credit card, or a loss of job might have prevented you from paying bills. On the other hand, maybe you are simply not diligent about keeping to a budget. If you want to get out of debt, you have to put your materialist desires aside and give money to the people you owe it to. Think of it as an act not so much of self-discipline as self-sacrifice. And as

HEXAGON

THE
FATHER'S
PROVISION

you give yourself up for others, you'll be amazed at how rich you'll feel.

*Dear Jesus, thank you for giving
to me so much even though you owe
me nothing. I am forever
in your debt. Amen.*

I WANT TO KNOW MY PURPOSE FOR LIFE

"'I have indeed seen the misery of my people
in Egypt.... So now, go. I am sending you
to Pharaoh to bring my people
the Israelites out of Egypt.'"

EXODUS 3:7;10

*J*ulie's high school reunion was coming up. She didn't know how she felt about it. Part of her was glad to show off pictures of her children and husband, but another part of her was ashamed to have no significant accomplishment to brag about. Already she had heard about several other classmates who had done amazing things: one was a doctor in a third-world country, one was a state senator, another was a novelist. She hadn't even accomplished her goal to lose ten pounds before the reunion. But she pushed all that insecurity away when she thought about how much she once loved these people. She knew that would never go away.

It seems as if God calls some people to specific tasks.

Those tasks may be of great significance or may be downright mundane. Some of us feel like we know exactly what God is calling us to and are delighted to be where God wants us to be—and then some great obstacle comes in to shatter that dream. Others of us feel like we're just plodding along in life without any clear direction from God—and we long for the faith that others seem to have. We want to know why we are here.

God does have a specific task for every single person who ever lived or who ever shall live. The fact that we all share the identical purpose does not minimize its importance: Your purpose is to praise God. He created this universe to give honor to him. He doesn't need you; he doesn't need angels or mountains or leviathans in order to have worth. But he chose to make us anyway. He wants you to live in his kingdom. As you devote your life to honor him, you find your reason for living, and your heart will fill with joy.

HEXAGON

THE
FATHER'S
KINGDOM

Almighty God, I honor you and
give you praise. You are worthy.
Glorify your name in all the earth.
Amen.

Additional copies of this and other Honor products
are available wherever good books are sold.

Other titles in this series:

God's Invitation to a Meaningful Life
A Passionate Life Devotional Journal

If you have enjoyed this book,
or if it has had an impact on your life,
we would like to hear from you.

Please contact us at:

Honor Books
Cook Communications Ministries, Dept. 201
4050 Lee Vance View
Colorado Springs, CO 80918

Or visit our Web site:

www.cookministries.com

HONOR ⟨HB⟩ BOOKS

Inspiration and Motivation for the Seasons of Life